Costa Rica Travel Guide

Captivating Adventures through Must-See Places, Local Culture, Landmarks, Hidden Gems, and More

© Copyright 2024 - All rights reserved.

The content contained within this book may not be reproduced, duplicated, or transmitted without direct written permission from the author or the publisher.

Under no circumstances will any blame or legal responsibility be held against the publisher or author for any damages, reparation, or monetary loss due to the information contained within this book, either directly or indirectly.

Legal Notice:

This book is copyright-protected. It is only for personal use. You cannot amend, distribute, sell, use, quote, or paraphrase any part of the content within this book without the consent of the author or publisher.

Disclaimer Notice:

Please note the information contained within this document is for educational and entertainment purposes only. All effort has been executed to present accurate, up-to-date, reliable, and complete information. No warranties of any kind are declared or implied. Readers acknowledge that the author is not engaging in the rendering of legal, financial, medical, or professional advice. The content within this book has been derived from various sources. Please consult a licensed professional before attempting any techniques outlined in this book.

By reading this document, the reader agrees that under no circumstances is the author responsible for any losses, direct or indirect, that are incurred as a result of the use of the information contained within this document, including, but not limited to, errors, omissions, or inaccuracies.

Welcome Aboard, Discover Your Limited-Time Free Bonus!

Hello, traveler! Welcome to the Captivating Travels family, and thanks for grabbing a copy of this book! Since you've chosen to join us on this journey, we'd like to offer you something special.

Check out the link below for a FREE Ultimate Travel Checklist eBook & Printable PDF to make your travel planning stress-free and enjoyable.

But that's not all - you'll also gain access to our exclusive email list with even more free e-books and insider travel tips. Well, what are you waiting for? Click the link below to join and embark on your next adventure with ease.

Access your bonus here:
https://livetolearn.lpages.co/checklist/
Or, Scan the QR code!

Table of Contents

INTRODUCTION 1
CHAPTER 1: GET TO KNOW COSTA RICA 4
CHAPTER 2: TO AND FROM THE AIRPORT 15
CHAPTER 3: SAN JOSÉ AND ITS DISTRICTS 20
CHAPTER 4: PUNTARENAS 30
CHAPTER 5: ALAJUELA 45
CHAPTER 6: GUANACASTE 58
CHAPTER 7: CARTAGO AND HEREDIA 73
CHAPTER 8: THE CARIBBEAN COAST (LIMON PROVINCE) 85
CHAPTER 9: ITINERARIES AND PROGRAMS 101
BONUS CHAPTER: USEFUL SURVIVAL PHRASES 127
APPENDIX 137
CONCLUSION 142
HERE'S ANOTHER BOOK BY CAPTIVATING TRAVELS THAT YOU MIGHT LIKE 145
WELCOME ABOARD, DISCOVER YOUR LIMITED-TIME FREE BONUS! 146
REFERENCES 147

Introduction

Costa Rica is a gem of Central America. The country's relative isolation throughout its history has allowed it to develop a unique identity that cannot be experienced anywhere else in the world. The captivating blend of colonial remnants, ancient archeology, and breathtaking biodiversity found nowhere else make Costa Rica a must-see destination on anybody's bucket list.

This guide to Costa Rica will give you in-depth insights into the country's different regions, outlining every aspect a visitor needs to know. Family-friendly destinations, entertainment, nightlife, natural wonders, culture, art, and dining experiences are all comprehensively covered in an easy-to-understand manner. Venturing into an unknown country is exciting but can also be intimidating. Therefore, this book will point you in the right direction so that you can fully enjoy your time in Costa Rica while easily overcoming the challenges of navigating the country and finding areas that fit your interests.

Costa Rica provinces.
https://commons.wikimedia.org/wiki/File:Costa_Rica_provinces_named.png

    This book sets itself apart from other travel guides by giving detailed explanations of all the country's treasures, which may pique your interest. Furthermore, it outlines all the logistics of travel, including how to easily get around in each region and what you can expect when you arrive. It also provides a complete list of accommodations for all income brackets. With this base understanding of the country, you can plant the seeds to cultivate a life-changing visit whether you plan to make the country home, spend a little time there for business, or explore the area as a tourist.

    This book contains all the basics you need to know about Costa Rica. This book covers everything, whether you want excitement, education, or relaxation. The labels are easy to follow, so you can jump to the exact section or category you are looking for. Instead of spending endless hours reading through every detail, you can navigate to what interests you and what fulfills your needs at that moment.

Take a chance and leap into the wonders of Costa Rica. Taste the blend of Spanish and indigenous influences as you breathe in the tropical air of sandy beaches and crystalline waters. Spend time amongst rural farmworkers, throw yourself into the hustle and bustle of the city, or explore the inspiring fauna and flora of the rainforests. The friendly people, beautiful weather, and ancient heritage are sure to leave a lasting impression. The country has depths of layers that keep unfolding new insights. This guide is your map to dig through the personality of Costa Rica, uncovering the magic of a peace-loving and diverse country.

NOTE: If listed, the normal operating hours were current as of the writing of this book, but please always double-check the hours online for any change in the attraction's schedule.

Chapter 1: Get to Know Costa Rica

You'll often hear, "You cannot leave Costa Rica the same way you came." The country has a magical way of profoundly shifting your narratives of what life is supposed to be all about. The blend of religion, indigenous practices, colonial heritage, and native customs creates a melting pot of art, culture, and cuisine that is truly eye-opening. The vibrant locals and natural beauty of the nation's diverse ecosystems will leave you awestruck. Imagine waking up in the morning to see a toucan perched on a tree and not on a cereal box. Costa Rica feels like you are stepping into a fairytale world straight out of the frames of a Pixar film. You've never seen color until you see Costa Rica.

Costa Rica has both history and luxury, depending on how you plan your trip.
https://www.needpix.com/photo/187633/

Costa Rica has it all, whether you want a foodie trip to all the local hole-in-the-wall spots or a luxurious spa overlooking pristine Caribbean waters. Marvel at colonial architecture or visit ancient ruins dating back to cultures thousands of years old. Dance to calypso as you Salsa the night to the upbeat rhythms that bang through the hearts of Costa Ricans. The deep heritage of this Central American haven is sure to echo in your mind for the rest of your life.

The country has issues with political polarization, a shaky economy, and increasing inequality. Still, the spirit of the locals has overcome far worse as the country established independence based on the identity developed in isolation. Unlike the past, Costa Rica is now open to the world, sharing the lessons it has learned through its ups and downs over thousands of years. Contemporary Costa Rica is finding a beautiful balance between urbanization and conserving its captivating flora and fauna as the locals sing the praises of an intimate bond with the land.

Costa Rica has many faces and cultures as you transition from the cramped city spaces to the volcanic shadows of agricultural land, into the undisturbed forest, and onto a tropical beach straight off the front of a postcard. Costa Rica tickles all your traveling fancies as a pristine destination for connection, self-discovery, and enjoyment on an indescribable level.

Geographical Location, Regions, and Provinces

Costa Rica is a nation located in Central America. The tropical region is humid and sunny most of the year and experiences heavy rainfall. The dry season is short, so the plants and animals are indicative of most tropical regions with lush green forests and colorful birds flapping about. You'll find interestingly diverse critters in every corner of the natural world integrated into the lifeblood of the country.

The nation is divided into seven provinces: Alajuela, Guanacaste, Cartago, Puntarenas, Heredia, Limón, and San José. Each of these provinces has a unique flag, identity, and culture, meaning there will also be new experiences to discover. Alajuela is best known for its rural feel and ecotourism but also has a growing industrial sector. San José International Airport is located in Alajuela. Cartago is the center of Costa Rica's colonial past. You can find many ruins from the colonial era in the province. Heredia is known for its natural beauty, including grasslands and amazing flowers. When you think of idyllic beachside living with warm winds and palm trees, Limón perfectly aligns with that vision. San José is the urban center of Costa Rica, and the government and many national monuments are hosted in the province. Puntarenas is home to Costa Rica's biggest port and one of the world's most biodiverse regions. Guanacaste is an agricultural hub with an abundance of volcanic ranges.

Despite the administrative functioning of the provinces, Costa Rica can be divided into six regions, including the Northern Lowlands, Central Pacific, Central Valley, North Pacific, Caribbean Coast, and South Pacific. Most of the population lives in the urbanized Central Valley, which is also a tourist's first experience of the country. The Northern Lowlands have gorgeous natural pools, which have encouraged a booming tourism industry. The Central Pacific has a mixed climate of wet and dry areas. The Northern Pacific has unique and iconic beaches. In contrast, the Caribbean Coast has sparkling blue water, white sand, and the most tropical feel of the country. Both the Osa Peninsula and the Nicoya Peninsula are in the South Pacific, which are some of the most biodiverse areas on the planet.

Background and History

The background of Costa Rica is the blending of two worlds: the deep traditions of the indigenous people of the land and the colonial Spanish who helped shape the country into what it is today. The colonial influence is evident in some of the historical buildings and churches, and the indigenous culture is not as prominent but is also a part of the country's identity through its customs, food, and crafts. Interestingly, Costa Rica has not had a military for about 68 years. The money saved by dismantling this institution has been used to build up various other aspects within the nation.

Unlike other countries in South America, many of the locals do not embrace the indigenous history of Costa Rica. The predominant influences of their culture come from their Spanish past, as well as their Catholic heritage. However, the region of Costa Rica was inhabited long before their Spanish colonialists entered the country. Some estimates say that humans have inhabited the region for over 5000 years. Costa Rica has had many ethnic influences throughout its history, including contributions from the Aztecs of Mexico and the Inca of Peru. Modernity and the Spanish influence have profoundly impacted Costa Rica, with the number of indigenous tribes still holding onto ancient traditions rapidly decreasing.

Costa Rica's road to independence and democracy was bumpy. They gained independence initially without much bloodshed. In 1855, William Walker entered the region intending to turn Central America into a slave territory. Juan Rafael Mora was the president of Costa Rica when William Walker implemented his plan. He put together an army of peasant forces who drove Walker into Nicaragua, mainly through the help of the brave Juan Santamaria, a drummer in the army who died bravely when he set fire to an enemy stronghold. San Juan Santamaria International Airport is named after this national hero. The peace brought on by Santamaria lasted until 1917, when the military dictator, General Federico Tinoco Granados, took over. In a crucial moment at the founding of the nation, a civil war was waged by Jose Figueres in which 2000 people died. The victory over the dictatorship caused the disbanding of the military.

'The Founding of the Country

Costa Rica has a rich history, and its founding makes for an epic story. Through a Eurocentric lens, Costa Rica was discovered in 1502 by the legendary and controversial Christopher Columbus. However, the area already had well-established civilizations with rich cultural traditions. The fertile land was named Costa Rica in 1502, which in English means Rich Coast. Ambitious colonialists thought that they would find gold in the hills.

Settlers in Costa Rica were isolated from other Spanish colonial hubs in the Americas, like Mexico and Guatemala, so they developed a unique agrarian culture of their own. At this time, the wealth of Costa Rica began growing due to the coffee and bananas the settlers cultivated that were well suited to the climate. In the process of clearing the land to make room for agricultural activities, European settlers found the ruins of an ancient culture. Today, the ruins are known as The Guayabo National Monument. The mysterious structures are estimated to date back to about 1000 BC and are believed to have been abandoned in about 1400 AD under unknown circumstances.

Costa Rica eventually gained independence from the Spanish Empire. Independence in much of Latin America came as the Spanish Empire began weakening after 1808 when the French conqueror Napoleon Bonaparte deposed the rulers of Spain. This caused the bricks of the Empire to start crashing in Latin America as calls for independence grew louder. Costa Rica was lucky to avoid the bloodshed that took place in Mexico and Peru from fighting the colonial powers. In 1821, after years of struggle, the whole of Central America gained its independence.

After Central America won independence, there was still conflict about how each of the territories in the region would be governed. These conflicts played out over the next few decades as Costa Rica fought for its complete independence. A 44-day Civil War following a disputed presidential election was the bloodiest in the country's history. José Figueres Ferrer led the uprising, which resulted in the abolition of the military and the drafting of a constitution. In 1953, José Figueres Ferrer was declared a national hero, and he is still honored to this day.

Relationships to Other Central American Countries

Costa Rica has a complex relationship with other countries in Central America. The country's isolation has enabled it to develop a unique identity, but it was a big player in regional events at times. One of the key moments was when Costa Rica was instrumental in bringing peace to a conflict-ridden region in 1987 under the leadership of President Oscar Arias Sanchez.

Although President Sanchez governed Costa Rica, which was experiencing economic issues with large foreign debt, he was also dedicated to bringing peace and stability to the war-torn region because he understood that this could bring prosperity to Central America as a whole. At the time President Oscar Arias Sanchez was in power, the Contra rebel forces supported by the United States in Honduras were attempting to overthrow Nicaragua's Sandinista government. Sanchez was critical of Nicaragua's government, but he never allowed the American-sponsored troops to make a base in Costa Rica despite the superpower applying immense pressure on him. Sanchez took the diplomatic route by crafting a peace plan for a ceasefire in the region, democratic elections, political prisoner exchanges, and cooperation, for which he won a Nobel Prize. The plan was never executed due to foreign intervention.

In Central America, Costa Rica has always stood as a diplomatic giant. The country has non-violently solved disputes with its neighbors and has even sent out olive branches to nations that were previously under sanctions, like Cuba. Therefore, the country's friendly attitude and peace-loving nature are not limited to individuals but extend through all its institutions, including the highest political office. According to the Global Peace Index, Costa Rica is ranked as the most peaceful Latin American nation, followed by Uruguay.

The country's lack of military, aversion to war and violence, and diplomatic prowess have framed it as a shining star in a region that can easily spiral into instability and chaos. The country has a stable democracy and emphasizes human and workers' rights. Furthermore, Costa Rica is a bastion of free speech in an area where many countries suppress their citizens' digital and communications freedom. Thus, Costa Rica stands as an example of progress and freedom that can be emulated all around the world.

Costa Rican Culture and People

Costa Rica is primarily made up of people of mixed heritage descending from the colonial Spanish and the region's indigenous people. The region's indigenous cultures include Cabécar, Maleku, Bribrí, Ngäbe, Huetar, Chorotega, Teribe, and Boruca. The eclectic mix of people is further diversified with immigrant groups from China, Jamaica, Italy, and Lebanon. 90% of the population speaks Spanish, and unfortunately, many of the indigenous languages are fading away as the youth become more modernized.

The general feel of Costa Rica is laid back and welcoming. The multicultural and multilingual country is vibrant and unrushed. The musical and cultural expression include colorful clothing, rhythmic instruments, and hypnotic dances that leave a lasting impact. There are minorities of Chinese who speak Cantonese, Jamaicans who speak a Creole dialect called Patois and English, and Mennonites who speak an interesting German variation called Plautdietsch.

Costa Ricans refer to themselves as Ticos or Ticas. They speak clear Spanish that is closely aligned with the original language, with a slight accent. About 10% of the local population probably speaks English as a second language due to the number of tourists frequenting the country. Like many other Latin American cultures, Costa Rican people predominantly subsist on rice, beans, and vegetables prepared in numerous interesting and delicious ways.

Catholicism is the state religion of Costa Rica, but religious freedom is respected in the country. Over 76% of the country identifies as Catholic as a result of Spain colonially exporting the religion. Almost 14% of the country are Evangelical Christians. Other religions like Judaism, Islam, Jehovah's Witnesses, and Protestant Christians are present as well but are not as prominent as Catholicism. Although their Catholic heritage is strong, many of the inhabitants of Costa Rica do not actively practice their religion and live more secular lives. Costa Ricans spend a lot of time with family and often come together for religious holidays and festivals. The national pastime is football, and their soccer team gets a lot of support from locals.

Cuisine, Art, Crafts, and Customs

Put aside the bacon and eggs. In Costa Rica, rice and beans are on the menu for breakfast. Gallo Pinto has rice and beans as the core of the dish, combined with lovely aromatic spices, onions, peppers, Salsa Lizano, and herbs to create a flavor explosion. The nation is known for its fresh, healthy ingredients that are not usually processed, coming straight from the field onto your plate. They eat a lot of seafood, fresh fruit, and vegetables prepared in hearty tropical dishes.

Although much of the local population is mixed with Spanish culture, the remaining two percent align closely with their indigenous roots, producing some of the world's most captivating arts and crafts. Local communities produce vibrant masks, intricate weaving dyed with natural plant materials, and beautiful vessels made with hardened fruit called jícaras. These jícaras are expertly crafted into unique designs of local wildlife.

Music is a central part of the rhythmic culture of Costa Rica. The older generation loves Latin music like Salsa, Soca, and Meringue, and this has also influenced younger people in the country. Many of the younger population enjoy Calypso and other Afro-Caribbean genres and sway their hips to the thumping beats. Costa Ricans also enjoy contemporary genres like Pop and Hip Hop. Dance flows through the blood of Costa Ricans as they visit dance halls on the weekends, move among family members, or participate in deeply rooted folk dances like Nicoyano, Punto Guanacasteco, Caballito, and El Torito.

Costa Rican culture is encapsulated in the ethos of Pura Vida, which translates to pure life in English. Essentially, the lifestyle of Pura Vida embodies a laid-back attitude and a value for hospitality as well as kindness to humanity and nature. The Pura Vida spirit of community is deeply woven into the Costa Rican identity and underpins many of the nation's ideals.

The mixed heritage of Costa Rica blends indigenous cultures with European traditions. The colonial architecture and Catholic influences give glimpses of Europe in the Latin American nation. Furthermore, the prominent language of the country is Spanish, which is spoken much like it is spoken in Spain. The native influences and the colonial identity blend in a way that creates a uniquely Costa Rican expression of self.

Sports and Leisure Activities

Costa Rica lives and breathes soccer, or as locals call it, "futbol." The nation comes to a standstill when important games are being played, especially those involving the national team. Locals call their beloved national team "La Sele" and give unwavering support. Children begin learning how to play from a young age, and amateur leagues and weekend mess-around games are commonplace, often getting super competitive. Local teams like Alajuela, Saprissa, and Heredia have huge fanbases, and games are often broadcast in pubs offering delicious and authentic Costa Rican cuisine.

Due to their connection with the water in this tropical region, Costa Ricans are avid swimmers and surfers. The beautiful weather year-round allows them to engage in these wonderful outdoor activities. In recent years, running and cycling have also become popular. Costa Rica also has a growing martial arts community with many small gyms in various areas. Taekwondo and Judo are particularly popular, with Costa Ricans often doing well in Latin American competition. The active nation keeps healthy and engages in many exciting activities for fun. Basketball has also gained some traction and is enjoyed by many people in the country, but it is still not as popular as it is in many other parts of the world.

The natural environment and sunny weather of Costa Rica facilitate many outdoor activities for locals and tourists alike. White water rafting and surfing are engaging options for those with a taste for adventure, and canopy zip lines are available for those looking for novel ways to experience the beauty of the plants and animal life in the country. Zip lines are hoisted up 50 feet in the air and began in a Quaker community in Monteverdi before spreading to other parts of the country. The southern regions of the country are best suited for water sports. Many locals also enjoy car racing. The racetrack in Guanacaste often hosts riveting races in a family-friendly environment that many Ticos and Ticas love.

Fishing is also a staple leisure activity in Costa Rica. The waters are filled with a wide variety of fish, including Tarpon, Wahoo, Dorado, and

Roosterfish. If you are worried about disrupting the local ecosystem, there is no need to fear because conservation efforts in the country have mandated that large game fish can only be caught on a catch-and-release basis.

Influential Costa Rican People

Costa Rica is a vibrant nation that has produced some spectacular people in history and the contemporary era. These people came from all walks of life, including art, politics, and entertainment. Their notable achievements have helped put Costa Rica on the map and brought a great sense of pride to their nation.

José María Hipólito Figueres Ferrer is one of the most iconic figures in Costa Rican history. The inspiring President served from 1948 to 1949, then again from 1953 to 1958, and from 1970 to 1974. President Ferrer governed the country through a gruesome Civil WAE and bolstered the dying economy during his last term, ushering Costa Ricans into an age of prosperity.

Juan Santamaria is the face of the Costa Rican revolutionary spirit. He died courageously defending his country against colonialism when William Walker invaded. He was shot dead while burning down Walker's hostel in an act of defiance. His death on April 11 is commemorated as the country remembers annually his heroic sacrifice for their freedom, independence, and self-determination.

When you move away from politics and into the realm of science, the name Franklin Chang Díaz will come up as one of the greatest minds of this century. The Costa Rican-American is an engineer, physicist, and astronaut who holds the record for the most space flights. He was born in Costa Rica and was later naturalized as a US citizen. Díaz currently runs the Ad Astra Rocket Company as President and CEO.

In the sports sphere, Claudia María Poll Ahrens deserves a mention as one of the most influential people from Costa Rica. Ahrens brought home the country's first Olympic gold medal for swimming. She won the country's first gold medal in 1988, then brought home the top prize again in 1996. In 2000, she earned 2 bronze medals. Ahrens was not only the first person in her country to win Olympic gold but also the first in the entirety of Central America to obtain the elite prize.

Francisco Amighetti is a Costa Rican artist who has gained international fame. His amazing work is influenced by European and American art and also incorporates elements of Japanese prints. In addition to painting, Amighetti has also made wooden carvings and has written beautiful poetry. The inspiration for his work comes from the way Costa Ricans live their lives and the complex, multilayered culture of the country.

Transportation, Tourism, and Accommodation

Costa Rica's public transport system can get you around anywhere in the country, but it is not as efficient as some European nations. The transport often gets delayed, so you will need to leave home well before you expect to reach your destination. The easiest and cheapest way to travel in Costa Rica is by using the bus system. Fees range anywhere from $5 to $20, depending on where you are going. It can be a little difficult to navigate the regional bus system, so you may have to consult some locals for assistance. The urban center of San Jose is the heart of the country's bus network.

You can also travel by taxi, and these can be identified by their distinctive red color. Taxis in Costa Rica are called "rojos" by the locals. Make sure you only use authorized taxi services for your own safety. There is a pandemic of unauthorized taxis known as "piratas." Legitimate taxis can be identified by the yellow triangle displayed on their doors. Unauthorized taxis are a little cheaper, but it is best to stick to well-established taxi companies. As a tourist, many people may want to take advantage of you. When you enter a taxi, check that the meter is running so you aren't overcharged.

Shared shuttles are another convenient way to travel. These mini-buses are comfortable, safe, and air-conditioned. They move around many corners of the country and are a great way to explore. These shuttles are more expensive than the buses. You can also opt to make use of the many tourist shuttle services in the country.

Renting a car is also a great option if you want to move around faster with no delays and more freedom. There are numerous reliable rental car services in the country, but make sure that you use a reputable company to acquire a car. The roads in Costa Rica can get a bit crazy, and there is a chance of falling victim to criminal elements, so remain vigilant and keep the doors locked when leaving the vehicle or while in congested areas. If you want to explore many parts of the country and move quickly between regions, domestic flights are also available. For an enjoyable, stress-free experience, you can enjoy a boat or ferry ride. The boats move between the country's coastlines and are a fun, relaxing way to spend a beautiful afternoon or enjoy the sunset.

Costa Rica is a lovely nation with many gorgeous accommodation options for all budgets. You can opt for mountain or beachside lodges or rent a cozy cabin isolated in nature for a romantic getaway. You can book into a luxurious hotel in the Caribbean, walk out of your door onto sandy beaches and clear blue water, or choose a more affordable option like a bed and breakfast among locals to submerge yourself in the interesting culture of the nation. As one of Central America's most popular tourist destinations, the options are endless.

Fun Facts about Costa Rica

- Although a wide array of animals in Costa Rica come to mind when you think of the tropical forest, like monkeys, predators, or spiders, the unexpected national animal is the two-toed and three-toed sloth. Although the white-tailed deer held this position for a long time, in 2021, the national symbol was changed to better represent the country.
- Costa Ricans are serious about conservation. There is a push to abolish zoos and create parks that are more reminiscent of natural habitats. They are also working to rehabilitate animals so that they can be released back into the wild.
- The country's weather is pleasant all year round, so you meet the tropical sun whenever you visit.
- As one of the country's most lucrative crops, coffee was foundational to establishing the country's strong standing in the globe.
- A variety of indigenous languages are spoken in the country by people belonging to one of the eight indigenous cultures found in Costa Rica. Sadly, with modernization, many of these languages are dying out.
- A Quaker village with its roots in the United States was established in Costa Rica in 1951. The group has helped with many of the country's conservation efforts.
- In Costa Rica, *soda* does not refer to a fizzy drink but is used as a term to describe small local eateries that serve dishes that the country is known for, like gallo pinto.

Chapter 2: To and From the Airport

There's nothing quite like that sigh of relief, knowing that you have landed safely, coupled with the excitement of getting off the plane to touch the soil of your destination. Your next step in an unknown country could be a little intimidating. You are probably unsure how to get to the next place and how the transport functions. This chapter will shine some light on what you can do and your options once you reach Costa Rica. You'll most probably land at Juan Santamaría International Airport, but there are also other airports you'll encounter if you take domestic flights to explore the country further. Therefore, you need information about navigating Costa Rica from all the main airports in the country so you are not confused when you arrive and know the protocol to follow.

Juan Santamaría International Airport's Role in Costa Rican Travel

The first place you'll touch down in Costa Rica will likely be Juan Santamaría International Airport. *Bernal Saborio from Costa Rica, CC BY-SA 2.0 <https://creativecommons.org/licenses/by-sa/2.0>, via Wikimedia Commons: https://commons.wikimedia.org/wiki/File:Mexicana_Airbus_A319_at_Juan_Santamaria_Internatio nal_Airport_(1).jpg*

The first place you'll touch down when you arrive in Costa Rica will likely be Juan Santamaría International Airport. The airport is about 19 kilometers from downtown San José, the most populated city in Costa Rica. The airport has direct flights from Europe, North America, and the other surrounding Central American countries. The airport is one of the busiest in the region, second only to Panama's Tocumen International Airport. This busy airport hosts many international and local airlines. Interestingly, before Liberia recently constructed Daniel Oduber Quirós Airport, Juan Santamaría International Airport was the only international gateway into the Guanacaste Province.

This airport connects to all major regions in the country and is a hub of seamless travel. From this airport, you can access all the main points a traveler would likely love to see, like the Central Pacific Coast,

Monteverde, and Caribbean Coast. The airport is located in Alajuela Province – just outside of San José – and has two terminals, one dealing with flights in and out of the country and the other focusing on domestic travel. The domestic terminal is used to link to Daniel Oduber Quirós International Airport, in addition to other destinations.

The comfortable airport has several places to shop, relax, and eat. It is also a great place to get a last-minute souvenir if you forgot to grab something for a loved one back home. The airport has restaurants where you can sit down and eat and fast food places to get a bite on the go if you are in a rush. AERIS Holding Costa Rica SA runs the logistics and administration, including overseeing the businesses in the airport. As soon as you land, you'll begin to experience the culture of Costa Rica with beautiful coffee shops and artists selling handmade crafts and paintings. Juan Santamaría International Airport is like a handshake welcoming you to Costa Rica.

Facilities, Logistics, and Transport Options

You might ask yourself what to do once you arrive at the airport. There are many options for you to explore, and there are helpful support desks that can point you in the right direction. You can book a low-cost shuttle to get you where you need to be or use the bus services that run at all hours of the day. Another option is renting a vehicle because car rental places are on the premises. If you are going to a destination that is a little bit too far to drive to, or you are on a tight schedule, you can book domestic flights that can take you all over Costa Rica. Most people make their way to the capital of San José when they first arrive, which is a good option because this central place connects to all parts of Costa Rica and is a brilliant place to begin engaging with the local sights, smells, and sounds in an urban and modern environment.

Traveling by taxi is the fastest way to get around. Taxis are also the most convenient way, and using one of the shared taxi services will not be excessively expensive. You can get a taxi straight from the airport to any destination you want to reach. A taxi from the airport to downtown San José will cost you $25 to $30. Buses are the cheapest way to travel, and because they are always running, you can use them at whatever time you arrive. Costa Rica is a relatively small country, so you can drive to any section of the land. If you take the option of renting a car, you should be aware that you need to be a highly skilled driver because many roads are damaged and ridden with potholes. Some roads in the country are narrow and on steep hills, so it can be dangerous if you are not accustomed to driving in these conditions.

Once you travel from the airport to San José, you will have access to all the major attractions in Costa Rica. Buses are by far the best way to travel, so once you are in the capital, you can study the bus schedule and plan accordingly. You can get a domestic flight from the airport to many of the regions in Costa Rica for as little as $60. The domestic airports in Costa Rica are Daniel Oduber Quirós International Airport, Tobías Bolaños International Airport, and Limón International Airport.

Daniel Oduber Quirós International Airport: Gateway to the Beaches of Costa Rica's Guanacaste Province

Regarding its importance for travel, this airport is only second to Juan Santamaría International Airport. International flights arriving at Daniel Oduber Quirós International Airport are popular because of the natural beauty of Guanacaste Province. The region's luxury resorts and iconic beaches attract tourists from all over the world, keeping this airport busy. The airport is about 88.5 kilometers from the Nicaraguan border and about 453 kilometers from the Panama border.

Daniel Oduber Quirós International Airport goes by many names and is referred to as *Liberia Costa Rica Airport* or *Liberia Airport* due to its proximity to the province's capital city. In some marketing material, it has also been called Guanacaste Airport, which distinguishes the city of Liberia from the African nation of the same name. You can reach Daniel Oduber Quirós International Airport by domestic flights, but some international airlines arrive directly at this destination. The airport is more rural than its urban cousin, Juan Santamaria International Airport, so you can easily reach it because the roads are straightforward. Once you arrive, you have the option of using buses, taxis, or even a car rental to get around the beautiful beaches of this stunning province.

Tobías Bolaños International Airport (SYQ): Domestic Flights

This airport is located in the Pavas district of San José and is named after a popular Costa Rican pilot. It is close to Juan Santamaría International Airport because they are both in the wider area of San José. The airport is not as big and busy as Juan Santamaría International or Daniel Oduber Quirós International Airport. It is about a 6-minute drive from the US embassy, so if you are an American traveler, it is convenient in case you experience any emergencies. Tobías Bolaños International Airport is the main hub of all domestic flights due to it being in the urban center of Costa Rica.

Typically, you would arrive at Juan Santamaría International and then make the short trip to Tobías Bolaños International, where you can catch a flight to many of the beautiful natural destinations in Costa Rica. Furthermore, there are shuttles available connecting the two airports. You also have the option of taking a taxi. Uber is available in the urban center as well. You can reach several domestic destinations from the airport, including Liberia, Nosara, Quepos, Tamarindo, La Fortuna, Drake Bay, or Puerto Jiménez. The airport also caters for flights to neighboring countries in Central America, like Nicaragua and Panama.

Limón International Airport (LIO): The Caribbean Connection

Costa Rica's Caribbean region is known for its white sandy beaches, crystal clear water, and tropical plant life, giving you that luxurious island feel. This airport is a couple of kilometers away from Puerto Limón. Limón International Airport is near the popular destinations of Cahuita National Park and Tortuguero in the Caribbean area of Costa Rica. If you enjoy the beach and are an avid surfer, this may be the first airport you would encounter. The tropical wildlife of the area is why many travelers opt to visit this region, so the airport is the gateway into the Caribbean.

The best time to travel using Limón International Airport is around Columbus Day, as locals will be celebrating the Dia de las Culturas festival. This festival is filled with colorful decorations and vibrant dances set to the backdrop of Caribbean and Latin music in a beautiful mesh of the country's cultures. The airport has recently started catering to international flights and was first used exclusively for domestic travel. You can use bus services or taxis to travel once you arrive, which are quite affordable, starting from as little as $4.

NOTE: Any hours provided for attractions were correct as of the printing of this book; please be sure to check hours ahead of time for the places you'd like to visit.

Chapter 3: San José and Its Districts

The first city/region chapter is devoted to the capital city, San José. It provides a well-rounded and informative introduction to San Jose, its historical background, and a comprehensive overview of the city's key attractions and landmarks, cultural experiences, and practical travel tips.

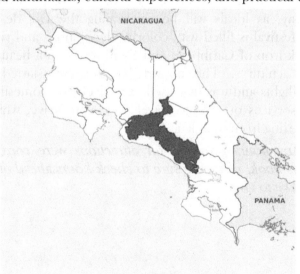

Named in honor of Jose of Nazareth, San Jose's rich historical tapestry plays a crucial role as Costa Rica's capital.
TUBS, CC BY-SA 4.0 <https://creativecommons.org/licenses/by-sa/4.0>, via Wikimedia Commons, https://commons.wikimedia.org/wiki/File:Costa_Rica,_administrative_divisions_-_de_-_monochrome.svg

Historical and Background Information about San José

Named in honor of Jose of Nazareth, San Jose's rich historical tapestry plays a crucial role as Costa Rica's capital. The first settlement, which later became the center of San Jose city, arose around 1738. Interestingly enough, San Jose wasn't always the capital city. When the Spanish conquistadors abandoned the Central American colonies in 1821, San Jose became Costa Rica's capital city for the first time. After a few months and due to some still inexplicable confusion, it ceased to be the capital until 1823, when it was once again appointed as the capital.

Due to the thriving coffee plantations, the city grew through the rest of the 19th century, slowly becoming a mixture of traditions and modernity. San Jose City expanded rapidly in the 1960s due to industrialization, which made it a very inviting prospect to the citizens of neighboring countries. When these newcomers began to arrive to work and live in Costa Rica, San Jose saw the rise of its tallest buildings so far, and much of the original population began to move toward the surrounding countryside.

Now, San Jose, known as Chepe by the locals, is the head of Costa Rica's Central Province and a powerful political and economic driving source in the country. Surrounded by mountains and fast streams, the city boasts fertile lands and lucrative companies, which facilitated it becoming the country's center of production for many products and services. Despite the idyllic natural surroundings, many locals in San Jose spend their days living a fast-paced, urban life as they work in the high office towers, malls, or establishments visited by tourists.

To avoid traffic jams, there are daily number plate prohibitions, which prevent drivers with certain plate numbers from driving on downtown roads. Unlike in many other countries where the roads are labeled with a name and number, the two types of roads in San Jose (avenues and streets) are labeled with even and odd numbers, respectively.

Officially, San Jose is composed of the San Sebastián, Pavas, San Francisco de Dos Ríos, Hatillo, Mata Redonda, Carmen, Zapote, Merced, Uruca, Catedral, and Hospital districts. Other crucial regions, known as Barrios, are Barrio Mexico, Barrio Amon Desamparados, Los Yoses, Escazu, Tibas, San Pedro, Moravia, San Bosco, and Rhomoser.

Did You Know?

The majority of San Jose's population lives outside the city center in the suburbs, giving the capital city a low population density. Despite this, thousands of people travel through San Jose every day, some tourists, while others use the city as a working environment. This makes San Jose Costa Rica's most important commercial hub.

Main Attractions

Did You Know?

San Jose is located in the Central Valley region of Costa Rica. It has quickly become a bustling city with more than a third of the country's population. Named in honor of Joseph of Nazareth, the city is the seat of the country's national government and an important point of political and economic activity. "When visiting San Jose, you are bound to experience some rainy days, as it rains 237 days out of the year. However, due to the high altitude, the humidity isn't accompanied by scorching heat (and you even have to put on a jacket during the colder months), which makes exploring the beautiful natural sights and historical landmarks even more convenient.

Some of the attractions and iconic landmarks of San Jose include the National Theatre, the Pre-Columbian Gold Museum, and Central Park. Central Avenue goes straight to downtown San Jose and takes you to every part of the city, including Central Park, making it the perfect starting point for sightseeing. Walking around the park after 5 in the afternoon, you'll see many locals enjoying a stroll to wind down after a busy day of work.

The Costa Rica National Theater.
Richie Diesterheftderivative work: MrPanyGoff, CC BY 2.0 <https://creativecommons.org/licenses/by/2.0>, via Wikimedia Commons: https://commons.wikimedia.org/wiki/File:National_Theatre_of_Costa_Rica.jpg

The Costa Rica National Theater is a true nation's gem that can be visited on guided tours or without a guide. The guided tour lasts about an hour and offers insights into the country's rich cultural past. If you decide to take a stroll on your own, you can pay the entrance fee at the door and wander through the place in about 30 minutes. After your tour, you can get snacks and drinks at the National Theater's lovely coffee shop if you get hungry or thirsty.

As of the writing of this book, the normal opening hours are from Mondays to Sundays from 9 AM to 5 PM, with guided tours being available from 9 AM to 4 PM daily. However, please always double-check the opening hours online should there have been any slight change in their schedule.

The Gold Museum offers a view of a massive collection of pre-Columbian gold findings.
Kenneth Lu, CC BY 2.0 <https://creativecommons.org/licenses/by/2.0>, via Wikimedia Commons: https://commons.wikimedia.org/wiki/File:Figures_at_the_Pre-Columbian_Gold_Museum_in_San_Jos%C3%A9,_Costa_Rica.jpg

Located under the Plaza de la Cultura, the enchanting Gold Museum offers a view of a massive collection of pre-Colombian gold findings dating back to AD 500.

As of the writing of this book, the normal opening hours are from Mondays to Sundays from 9:15 AM to 4:30 PM. However, please always double-check the opening hours online should there have been any slight change in their schedule.

Transport

Did You Know?

While tourists arrive in San Jose (and Costa Rica in general) through the San Jose International Airport, many are shocked to find that this airport is around 20 minutes away from the city in a town called Alajuela. The reason behind this is simple. San Jose, although known for its natural beauty, has a very difficult terrain, making building a massive international airport impossible.

How you choose to get around San Jose is one of the crucial decisions you'll make when planning your dream Costa Rican vacation. It all depends on your budget, comfort needs, and travel preferences. Lack of airports notwithstanding, San Jose has a well-maintained public transport system, which makes getting around the city very easy. Shuttles are a fantastic option if you prefer not to drive while on vacation or if renting a car isn't within your budget. San Jose has several local shuttle routes and affordable departure routes to different areas of the country. They take you to and from airports and destinations in vehicles with comfortable seating, which isn't guaranteed on public buses. Still, the public bus system is also a budget-friendly variant many tourists prefer, especially on short journeys. Routes and stops are scattered throughout the city, and if you have trouble gauging which one to board or when yours will arrive, check with the locals, as they are always there to give you friendly advice.

If you're traveling by car, you'll be happy to learn that the main attractions are a short distance from lodgings, eateries, and other amenities. However, when renting a car, make sure you purchase the mandatory car insurance, which, although required by the Costa Rican government, isn't included in the primary booking price. If you prefer taking a taxi, the go-to company in San José is Taxi Rojo (red taxi). You'll find these fire-engine red taxis everywhere, and they're fairly effortless to flag down. The city itself is usually defined by the borders of San Pedro and La Sabana, a distance of less than 8 kilometers, which you can cover easily by car (rented or taxi).

San Jose also offers plenty of biking opportunities, and you can also explore the city on foot and experience local life. Even walking leisurely, you can cover the city in about two hours, and heading from one landmark to another is often easier on foot or bike than with a car or public transport. The city has an intricate layout, where charming homes embody the local culture, which tourists traveling by car often miss.

Experiences

Among the most popular activities for tourists visiting Costa Rica's capital are day trips and tours from San Jose. Some of the most recommended options are trips to areas like Arenal Volcano, Poas Volcano, and Tortuguero National Park. There are numerous tour companies where you can book your trip.

Poas Volcano, known for its massive and stunning acid-blue lake crater, is a very active volcano about an hour and a half's drive from San Jose city center. As one of the world's biggest craters, the tour of the volcano is typically the number one thing to do for visitors. It is recommended that you take the earliest tour available, the Poas Volcano National Park Half-day tour from San Jose, which starts at 8 am, as you'll avoid waiting in long lines. You'll only have to pay the tour fee, and the entrance to the volcano area is free.

A 45-minute drive from San José airport is La Paz Waterfall Gardens, the largest private wildlife sanctuary in Costa Rica. Walking on the park trails, you can see white rivers, thundering cascades, the White Magic Waterfall, snakes, and other creatures of the picturesque, lush Costa Rican rainforests, as well as colorful butterflies in the butterfly observatory. To combine the visit to the sanctuary with other experiences, book an organized day tour from San Jose, which includes a guided walk through the park, lunch, and transport to and from La Paz.

You can't leave San Jose without trying the worldwide renowned Costa Rican coffee brewed from beans grown in one of the country's hundreds of plantations. You can experience local coffee making through a coffee tour like the Britt Coffee tour in Heredia, which is a 9-mile drive away from the San Jose center. It includes tasting the most delicious caffeine-rich brews and chocolate, lunch, and transportation to and from San Jose.

Located near the neighboring town of La Fortuna, Arenal Volcano is another one of San Jose's top attractions. The full-day Hanging Bridges, La Fortuna Waterfall, and Arenal Volcano Hike tour will take you on an eventful and active journey across a hanging bridge, the volcano area, and the picturesque La Fortuna Waterfall.

Besides La Fortuna, you can also chase other waterfalls like Rio Celeste. The easiest way to explore this waterfall is through the Rio Celeste Waterfall at Tenorio Volcano and the Sloth Watching Tour from San Jose (booked in San Jose).

Wildlife lovers can peek into the lives of Costa Rica native animals at the Manuel Antonio National Park through the highly popular Manuel Antonio Park Nature Guided Tour, which offers amazing views. Tortuguero National Park is another place where you can observe Costa Rican wildlife in its natural habitat, while the Rescate Wildlife Rescue Center in San Jose also offers private tours.

Family Fun

If you're visiting the city with your children, you'll be able to choose from many family-oriented programs, including a visit to the Children's Museum. There are also amusement parks, such as Parque Diversiones, which are worth investigating.

Address: WWR9+GR4, Av 9, San José, Bajos de La Union, Costa Rica

Interestingly enough, the Children's Museum was once a prison but now offers cultural presentations, science exhibitions, and hands-on demonstrations where people of all ages can learn about Costa Rica's fascinating past. Little archeologists will also enjoy exploring the Jade Museum, which has over 7,000 American jade artifacts on display. This museum is located at the Plaza de la Democracia.

Where to Eat

Did You Know?
San Joseans' favorite food, Gallo Pinto, a mixture of black beans and fried rice, is also Costa Rica's official national dish. They love it so much that you'll see working people with lunchboxes of Gallo Pinto.

San Jose is famous for its unique local dining and cuisine experiences. Regarding recommendations on eateries to visit, you'll find the best traditional dishes like Gallo Pinto, Casado, or Sopa Negra at most restaurants in San Jose.

Besides being a popular meeting point, Restaurante Nuestra Tierra offers the best Costa Rican and Central American dishes in San Jose. This trendy restaurant is located next to the Plaza de la Democracia 'and serves meals made from locally sourced and fresh ingredients. It's great for brunch!

Address: Avenida Segunda, frente a la Plaza de la Democracia, Av. 2, San José, Costa Rica

Ram Luna is the restaurant with the best view in the city, as it is set over 5,000 feet above sea level. It's a family-owned place where you can enjoy local dishes while listening to live music or enjoying a dance show and winding down with a glass of wine or beer. You can also enjoy the stunning views of the mountains or the nearby Irazú Volcano and the cities of Tres Ríos, Heredia, Aserrí, and San Jose itself.

Address: San José Province, Aserrí, Costa Rica

If you're looking for the best breakfast place in San Jose, head to Franco Escalante. Here, you can enjoy the best of Costa Rican coffee, and after waking up your senses, you can fill up on the various egg combinations, smoothies, local breakfast options, and much more. Have your breakfast/brunch/lunch on the patio or garden area, where you can relax in a flowery and fresh atmosphere. A spacious indoor seating area welcomes the arriving guests if the weather is bad.

Address: Entre Calles, Av. 7 3166, San José Province, CARMEN, Barrio Escalante, 10101, Costa Rica

Located in the Grano de Oro Hotel's central courtyard, Restaurante Grano de Oro offers the best fine dining experience in the city. Here, you can relax with the best of the local and international cuisine (including some of the best French dishes you'll taste in Costa Rica), which you can pair with coffee or a premium cocktail or wine.

Address: WWM4+CQQ, Calle 30, San José, San Bosco, 10101, Costa Rica

In the heart of San Jose is the delightful and budget-friendly Café Rojo, offering a mixture of fusion, healthy local, and Vietnamese cuisine. This mansion-turned-restaurant is a trendy coffee shop that became a much-loved cultural space for celebrating diversity. The place also offers great coffee and spicy beverages to spruce up those rainy days you will eventually encounter during your stay.

Shopping Guide

Popular shopping centers in San Jose include Multiplaza, Avenida Escazú, and Plaza Real Cariari. You can also visit shopping districts like San Pedro, Escazú, and Santa Ana for an even better shopping experience.

If you are up for some souvenir shopping, a visit to the Municipal Craft Market is a must. Here, you'll find colorful artisanal products made by local artists.

Address: Calle 5 y 7, Avenida 6, in front of al Parque de las Garantías Sociales, San José, Capital, 10104, Costa Rica

If you want an authentic Costa Rican shopping experience, head to the San Jose Central Market, where you can see locals shop around, bargain, and go about their daily lives. At the same time, you can do some shopping of your own and try traditional delicacies made on-site.

Address: WWM9+V5F, Calle 8, San José Province, San José, Paso De La Vaca, Costa Rica

Entertainment

San Jose boasts a rich cultural scene, including numerous museums, theaters, and music venues. Those looking for something fun to do after a long day of exploring or activities can choose from several entertainment options. San Jose is notorious for its fantastic nightlife — not to mention the festivals that you can catch if you visit at the right time.

Held on August 2nd, Virgin of Los Angeles Day is a monumental religious festival in Costa Rica. Thousands of people from across the country gather at the capital city of San Jose and embark on a journey to finish the ceremony held in honor of their patron saint at the Basilica Church in Cartago, located 22.5 kilometers away.

The Lantern Parade is held on September 14th as part of a two-day Independence celebration across the country. If you're visiting the Costa Rican capital in December, you can't miss the Festival de la Luz (Light Festival), which starts the festive season at the Paseo Colon in downtown San Jose. This highly popular event incorporates floats, mask-wearing artists and dancers, displays of magic, fireworks, and live music, which travels across the entire city.

Sports and Leisure

If you feel adventurous and love water sports, try whitewater rafting on the Pacuare River. Take a White Water Rafting Pacuare River Full Day Tour from San Jose, and you'll have a view of the tropical rainforest the river crosses while having the most epic day full of fun experiences.

By embarking on a 10-day Surf Costa Rica from San Jose tour, you can enjoy the great waves and miles of white sandy beaches and see beautiful water wildlife while surfing.

Accommodations

San Jose offers accommodation options for various budgets, including hotels, hostels, and other unique accommodations. For example, Hotel Cultura Plaza has an excellent location at affordable prices. It's close to the shopping street of San José, less than half a mile from the Jade Museum and the Costa Rica National Museum, and at walking distance from the Pre-Colombian Gold Museum. The nearest airport is Tobías Bolaños International, a little under 8 kilometers from the accommodation, and the hotel offers a paid airport shuttle service.

Address: Calle 5 Av Primera y al frente de Cine Variedades San José, 10101, Costa Rica

Studio Hotel Boutique is a higher-budget option but offers a celebrity treatment with a rooftop swimming pool, eco-friendly amenities, and an à la carte restaurant. The property is in the middle of the Santa Ana district and features a view of the surrounding Central Valley. You can enjoy a buffet breakfast and choose from the range of international cuisines in the Studio's restaurant.

Address: 50 metros Norte de la Cruz Roja, San José, Santa Ana, 10901, Costa Rica

Chillout Hostel Barrio Escalante offers plenty of budget-friendly and sustainable options, including shared amenities, a spacious terrace, allergy-free rooms, and a bicycle rental service. You can also book airport transfers at the hostel. Tobías Bolaños International Airport is slightly over 12 kilometers away, while Estadio Nacional de Costa Rica is around 10 kilometers from the hostel.

Address: Calle 37, 75m south of Sapporo Restaurant, San José, Barrio Escalante, 10101, Costa Rica

Boasting a spacious shared lounge and kitchen and a beautiful garden view, Stray Cat Hostel is less than a mile away from the center of San Jose. It is located 3.5 kilometers from La Sabana Metropolitan Park and 8 kilometers from Tobías Bolaños International Airport, to which you can book a transfer at the hostel's front desk. Other landmarks close to the property include Poas National Park, Parque Diversiones, Estadio Nacional de Costa Rica, Alejandro Morera Soto Stadium, Jardin Botanico Lankester, and Parque Viva.

Address: En la Escina, Av. 9 905, San José, Barrio México, Costa Rica

Chapter 4: Puntarenas

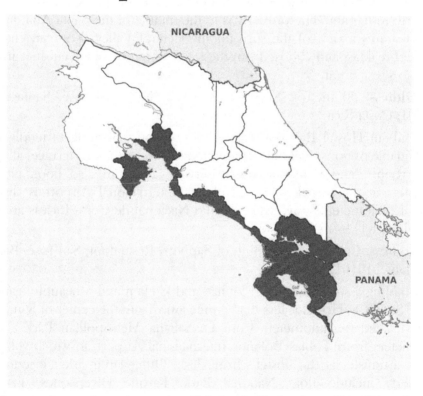

Puntarenas is a popular tourist attraction with its breathtaking beaches and beautiful scenery.
TUBS, CC BY-SA 4.0 <https://creativecommons.org/licenses/by-sa/4.0>, via Wikimedia Commons, https://commons.wikimedia.org/wiki/File:Costa_Rica,_administrative_divisions_-_de_-_monochrome.svg

Many people think that Guanacaste is the largest province in Costa Rica. However, Puntarenas holds this honor. It is 4,350 square miles and consists of 11 cantons. It is the home to Jaco Beach and Manuel Antonio, the most famous cities in the country. It is a popular tourist attraction with its breathtaking beaches and beautiful scenery.

This chapter covers Puntarenas' history, main attractions, popular restaurants, and fun facts to see why this will be the trip of a lifetime.

Historical and Background Information about Puntarenas

In 1519, conquistador Hernán Ponce de León first laid eyes on Puntarenas during the Spanish colonialism era but never attempted to land. It was Gil González Dávila who laid claim to the land in 1522 when he arrived on foot. It was isolated from the rest of the country for years because it wasn't easily accessible. However, it served as a gateway and port to the Gulf of Nicoya.

In 1720, the province was called Punta de Arena, but over the years, it came to be known as Puntarenas. In 1858, it became a city and Costa Rica's main port. It also played a major role in the rise of the country.

Many countries worldwide, such as Nicaragua, Panama, and China, influenced Puntarenas" culture. The city was famous for its hard-working, friendly, and sociable citizens. Puntarenas was one of the world's main coffee exporters, contributing to the expansion of its economy. However, now it relies on tourism and is known for its commercial fishing port.

Puntarenas' capital is Puntarenas City, and it is located in Nicoya Gulf. Tourists enjoy the city's liveliness, urban beaches, and waterfront cafes and restaurants. It also has more parks and reserves than any other province. Puntarenas is also the home to Cocos Island, also called Isla del Coco, one of Costa Rica's largest and most famous national parks (around 550 kilometers southwest of the mainland), with some of the most magnificent and dense tropical rainforests.

Thanks to its beautiful beaches, islands, rivers, and many famous protected areas, it has become the country's most popular tourist attraction. People go there to enjoy a quiet, relaxing, and fun holiday while taking in the city's natural scenery.

Did You Know?

- Puntarenas isn't a historic city and doesn't have many ancient sights.
- The highest mountain in Puntarenas is Cerro Dúrika.
- People from Puntarenas are called Puntarenense.

Main Attractions

Puntarenas has many tourist attractions, making it a favorite destination for people from all over the world.

Montezuma Waterfalls

One of the Montezuma Waterfalls.
Vlad Podvorny, CC BY-SA 3.0 <https://creativecommons.org/licenses/by-sa/3.0>, via Wikimedia Commons: https://commons.wikimedia.org/wiki/File:Waterfall_in_Montezuma_-_panoramio.jpg

Montezuma Waterfalls are a set of three magnificent waterfalls that are Puntarenas' main attraction. The smallest one is on the top, perfect for jumping and swimming. You will find a rope hanging from a tree to swing on and hurl yourself into the water.

You can only reach the middle waterfall through the top one. You don't need transportation and can just swim until you get there. However, the second waterfall isn't safe for jumping, so just enjoy the view. Be very careful when on the edge because the rocks are slippery.

The biggest waterfall is the most popular one. You will always find tourists there. Don't miss the opportunity to take a swim in its beautiful pool. Avoid jumping because there are many dangerous rocks in the water.

You can enter Montezuma Waterfalls through the Riverbed Trial or SunTrails entrance.

Opening Hours: 24/7.

Santa Teresa Beach

Santa Teresa Beach.
Vixitaly, CC BY 3.0 <https://creativecommons.org/licenses/by/3.0>, via Wikimedia Commons: https://commons.wikimedia.org/wiki/File:Playa_Santa_Teresa_-_panoramio_(1).jpg

If you love surfing, Santa Teresa Beach should be on your itinerary. It is located in a remote area in one of the quietest parts of Puntarenas, away from the city's noise and light. This beach is one of the most exciting places you will visit. You will find hip restaurants, beach parties, and many other fun events.

This beach has also been a favorite destination among many celebrities like Tom Brady. People from around the world visit it to surf on its one-of-a-kind beach. However, the strong currents and high waves sometimes make swimming and surfing challenging. In this case, you can sunbathe or enjoy its gorgeous sunset.

Opening Hours: 24/7.

Did You Know?

- Before it became a surfing destination, Santa Teresa was a fishing village.
- There wasn't electricity in Santa Teresa until 1996.

Monteverde Cloud Forest Reserve

Monteverde Cloud Forest Reserve.
*User: (WT-shared) Velorian at wts wikivoyage, CC BY-SA 1.0
<https://creativecommons.org/licenses/by-sa/1.0>, via Wikimedia Commons:
https://commons.wikimedia.org/wiki/File:Cloud_Forest_at_Monteverde.JPG*

Monteverde Cloud Forest Reserve is an enchanting place that looks like it came out of a fairytale. With its hazy mist, mysterious sounds of exotic birds, and out-of-this-world natural scenery, the Monteverde Cloud Forest Reserve is on many people's bucket lists. So why is this forest so popular?

As their name implies, cloud forests have low-hanging clouds hovering over them, giving a foggy appearance. It looks like the sky fell over the forest, creating the impression that you are walking through the clouds.

The Monteverde Cloud Forest Reserve was established in 1972 and is home to 1,200 reptile species, 400 bird species, and 100 mammal species, many of which are endangered and rare.

Follow the signs at Santa Elena to find the entrance.

Opening Hours: 7 am to 4 pm.
Did You Know?
- Although there are other cloud forests in Costa Rica and other countries around the world, the Monteverde Cloud Forest Reserve is the most famous one.
- It is famous for bird watching since it is the home of many exotic birds like hummingbirds, toucans, bellbirds, and trogons.

Tarcoles Crocodile Bridge

If you're headed to Jaco, be sure to stop at the Tarcoles Crocodile Bridge. This interesting and free-to-visit place is the home to many fascinating animals, specifically the crocodiles that earned the bridge its name.

When walking on the bridge, you will see many crocodiles enjoying the sun or swimming. Los Pascos from Earth, CC BY-SA 2.0 <https://creativecommons.org/licenses/by-sa/2.0>, via Wikimedia Commons: https://commons.wikimedia.org/wiki/File:Toothy_Indulgence_(24978586824).jpg

When walking on the bridge, you will see many crocodiles enjoying the sun or swimming. After touring the place, you can have lunch at Restaurant Nambi, which is famous for its delicious food and strong coffee. There are also a few shops in the area if you want to buy souvenirs for your friends and family.

The bridge is around 26 kilometers north of Jaco.

Did You Know?
- Tarcoles River is one of the most polluted rivers in the country.
- All the wildlife in the city depends on this river.
- The river is responsible for generating electricity and agriculture.

Manuel Antonio National Park

Manuel Antonio National Park has everything from rainforests to beaches.
Sunset Sails, CC BY 4.0 <https://creativecommons.org/licenses/by/4.0>, via Wikimedia Commons: https://commons.wikimedia.org/wiki/File:Manuel_Antonio_National_Park_from_the_sea_08.jpg

Manuel Antonio National Park has everything from rainforests to beaches. There isn't a dull moment in the park. Although it is the smallest park in Costa Rica, it has become one of the country's main attractions. People visit it to get a glimpse of its hundred bird species, agoutis, iguanas, sloths, monkeys, squirrels, howler monkeys, and Capuchin monkeys.

The park only accepts 1,200 visitors every day. Book the early morning tour if you don't like crowds and want to explore the place in peace. The park is also famous for its beautiful beaches like Espadilla Sur and Escondido Beach.

There are also interesting beaches outside the park, like Playa Espadilla and Playa Manuel Antonio. You can do many fun activities on these beaches, like having fresh drinks, taking surfing lessons, buying souvenirs, or going parasailing.

The main entrance is located 7 kilometers miles east of Quepos.

Opening Hours: Every day from 7 am to 4 pm except Tuesday when it is closed.

Did You Know?

- Ponce de León, the Spanish explorer who was obsessed with the fountain of youth, is associated with the park. It is one of the few places where you can find endangered animal species like the squirrel monkey.

Transportation

You can easily explore Puntarenas either on foot or through its various methods of transportation.

Shared Shuttle

Shared shuttles involve you riding with other people. If you don't mind the company, you should consider this option since it is cheaper than other transportation methods. They usually take tourists to famous destinations like Monteverde or Manuel Antonio. These shuttles are usually air-conditioned and include WiFi.

Private Vehicles

Book a private vehicle if you want to splurge and spoil yourself. You can easily get to any place you want without wasting your time on public transportation. This option is better than renting a car since you will have a driver to take you wherever you want. These vehicles are comfortable and air-conditioned. They are perfect for taking you to the airport, so you won't worry about missing your flight.

Taxis

Taxis are one of the most common methods of transportation in Puntarenas. There are many taxis in Costa Rica, so you can easily find one that will take you anywhere around the city! Taxis are better and more accessible than buses. Make sure to tell the driver to turn on their meter because many take advantage of tourists and overcharge them.

Buses

Buses are extremely popular in Puntarenas. They are inexpensive, navigable, and reliable. They operate on set routes and a specific schedule. However, they are slow and will take longer than any other method of transportation to reach your destination.

Experiences

There are many fun experiences that you can enjoy in Puntarenas. Make sure you check these tours while you are there.

Zip Lining

If you are looking for a fun and safe adventure, you should go zip lining in Puntarenas. One of the most popular tours is from Santa Teresa and Mal País. Many companies will pick you up from your hotel or Airbnb to take you to Cabo Blanco Natural Reserve. You will zip-line across the tropical forest and enjoy the gorgeous ocean view, various bird species, and huge trees.

The adventure takes about 90 minutes to complete.

Hanging Bridge Hiking Tour

Monteverde is the perfect place for hiking. The Hanging Bridge Tour is unlike anything you will ever experience. You will walk on a hanging bridge that feels like you are walking in the clouds. Don't worry; this bridge is very safe, and this tour is suitable for people of all ages so you can enjoy the experience with your family. The tour takes about two hours.

Natural History Hiking Tour

If you are looking for a regular hike, take the natural history hike at Monteverde with a guide. These tours are usually private, so you will have the guide's undivided attention, and you can ask them anything you want about Monteverde and its history. The guide will show you wildlife like monkeys, sloths, and birds. They will also inform you about the animals and the country's ecosystem. This tour is available for people in wheelchairs as well.

Since these tours are private, the start times are flexible.

Jaco Horseback Riding

Do you love horseback riding? Jaco offers two-hour horseback riding tours in its lush forests and beautiful beaches. You will go on an epic journey and experience Puntarenas's natural scenery. You will feel like you have traveled back in time and are on an epic adventure. You will enjoy Jaco's wildlife and see monkeys, sloths, and colorful scarlet macaws.

If you have never ridden a horse before, don't worry. You will find different horses to match your riding experience. These tours are safe, and the horses are gentle and well-trained. Many of the tours are tailored to your preferences and interests.

Family Fun

If you are traveling with your family, you will find many fun activities you can enjoy together.

NATUWA Wildlife Sanctuary

Children love animals. To give your family the adventure of a lifetime, you should visit the NATUWA Wildlife Sanctuary. The place offers guides that will tell you about their different rehabilitation programs and wildlife. You will get a glimpse of wild animals like jaguars, margays, and two-toed sloths. You will also see different bird species like African gray parrots, toucans, and macaws. The sanctuary is located in the Pitahaya district.

As of the writing of this book, the sanctuary is open every day from 8 am to 4 pm. Guided tours are available all day. Please double-check those times.

Address: 1km Plaza deportes Santuario NATUWA, Provincia de Puntarenas, Pitahaya, 60102, Costa Rica

Parque Marino del Pacifico

Parque Marino del Pacifico is the only marine park in the country.
Rodtico21, CC BY-SA 3.0 <https://creativecommons.org/licenses/by-sa/3.0>, via Wikimedia Commons: https://commons.wikimedia.org/wiki/File:Parque_Marino_del_Pac%C3%ADfico,_Puntarenas,_Costa_Rica_(2).JPG

This adventure is for marine animal lovers. Parque Marino del Pacifico is the only marine park in the country. You will get the chance to see 50 types of marine and coastal creatures that were either rehabilitated or rescued. It is located at Paseo de los Turistas, an eight-minute walk from the main bus terminal.

As of the writing of this book, opening hours are Tuesday to Sunday from 9 am to 4:30 pm. Please double-check the hours before visiting.

Address: P.º de los Turistas, Provincia de Puntarenas, Puntarenas, Barrio Las Playitas, Costa Rica

Where to Eat

One of the most exciting parts about traveling is trying different cuisines. Luckily, you will find a variety of local and international restaurants in Puntarenas.

El Novillo Alegre Jaco

If you are looking for a mouthwatering steak meal, look no further than El Novillo Alegre Jaco. Located in Jaco, the restaurant offers Argentinian high-quality grilled meat and various other dishes like empanadas, milanesa, and vegetarian options.

Address: Calle Hiaco Hicaco Street, Jaco, Garabito Municipality 61101, Costa Rica.

La Junta Dominical

Puntarenas is famous for its beaches, as well as its food. La Junta Dominical offers fresh ingredients to satisfy your fish craving. It also has a diverse menu of salads, tacos, beef, kid meals, and seafood.

Address: In front of the Soccer Field, Dominical, Costa Rica.

Claro Que Si Seafood Restaurant

Claro Que Si Seafood Restaurant is perfect for couples. You will not get enough of this place with its romantic view and mouthwatering dishes. The menu offers local and international cuisine. However, it is mainly famous for its seafood dishes.

Don't leave right away after your meal. Stay and watch the sunset. The view will give you an intimate and unique experience.

Address: Manuel Antonio National Park Hotel Si Como No, Manuel Antonio, Quepos Costa Rica.

Rico Tico Jungle Grill Restaurant

Rico Tico Jungle Grill is another restaurant that has a fantastic view. It offers a casual and unique dining experience on a terrace at the heart of

Manuel Antonio's jungle. The restaurant prides itself on being sustainable and healthy. You will find a variety of dishes like seafood, pasta, and burgers.

Address: Hotel Si Como No Provincia de Puntarenas Manuel Antonio, 60601, Costa Rica

Shopping Guide

If you want to go shopping in Puntarenas and buy souvenirs for yourself and your friends, check out these popular stores.

Tico Pod Art House and Gifts

Art lovers should visit Tico Pod Art House and Gifts. This unique store offers hand-picked and unique gifts that will put a smile on your friends' and family's faces. You will find many Costa Rican products and art by local artists, like folk art, hand-made soaps, wood carvings, silver jewelry, and art canvas.

Address: Pastor Diaz Ave, Puntarenas Province, Jaco, Costa Rica.

Jaco Walk Open Air Shopping Center

Jaco Walk Center is located in the heart of Jaco Beach and is one of the most popular malls in the city. It is home to many stores, so you will find all your needs in one place.

Address: Frente a calle Alice Jaco Walk, Local 99 Puntarenas Jacó, 61101, Costa Rica.

Jungle Avenue

Jungle Avenue is a popular clothing store that sells stylish outfits, accessories, and swimwear for women. The brand prides itself on making comfortable, trendy, casual, and sexy clothes. If you are looking for elegant and unique outfits, visit Jungle Avenue.

Address: Plaza Vista, Provincia de Puntarenas, Quepos, 60123, Costa Rica

Altair Souvenir and Gallery Shop

In Altair Souvenir and Gallery Shop, you will find various local products like jewelry, lighters, coffee beans, art, and t-shirts. Check this place to shop for unique items and buy your friends lovely gifts.

Address: Puntarenas Province, Quepos, 60601, Costa Rica.

N.B. All the opening hours are accurate at the time of writing this book. However, please always double-check the opening hours online should there have been any slight change in their schedule.

Accommodations

You will find many hotels to stay in during your vacation that offer excellent services and fantastic views.

Lapoint Surf Camp Costa Rica Hotel

This hotel offers everything you are looking for to have your dream vacation. It is surrounded by natural scenery and a lush jungle. You will wake up to the sound of birds singing and can have breakfast while enjoying a beautiful and relaxing view. It offers a bar, pool, and a hammock to lie down and unwind.

Address: Playa Carmen, Santa Teresa, Mal Pais Cobano, 60111, Provincia de Puntarenas, Cobano, 60111, Costa Rica

Hotel Cayuga

This hotel is a national icon and has been renovated to provide guests with a relaxing and enjoyable experience. You can swim in the pool or have a delicious and refreshing drink from the hotel's mini-bar.

Address: Calle 4, Puntarenas Province, Puntarenas, Barrio Las Playitas, 60101, Costa Rica.

Hotel La Punta

If you want a peaceful and private holiday, La Punta is the hotel for you. Although it is in the middle of the city, the hotel is famous for its magnificent view of its large and beautiful gardens. It offers everything to accommodate you, like amenities, cable TV, and air conditioning. Whether you are spending your vacation alone or with your family, you will enjoy your stay at La Punta.

Address: 75 meters east of San Lucas Beach Club, Provincia de Puntarenas, Puntarenas, Costa Rica.

Posada Natura

Posada Natura is a healing sanctuary located in the rainforest. Take a journey inside yourself and discover what ails your spirit, mind, and body so you can heal. Immerse yourself in their sacred space by the river and take in the tropical beauty surrounding you.

Posada Natura serves vegetarian, fresh, and organic home-cooked meals to nourish your body and mind.

Address: Posada Natura, Provincia de Puntarenas, Naranjito, Londres, Costa Rica.

Key Areas

- **Montezuma:** Known for its picturesque beaches, waterfalls, and laid-back bohemian vibe, Montezuma is a paradise for those seeking relaxation alongside nature. It's perfect for eco-tourists, with opportunities for yoga retreats and organic cuisine. Take advantage of the stunning Montezuma Waterfalls for a refreshing dip or a scenic picnic.
- **Santa Teresa:** With its consistent waves, Santa Teresa is a haven for surfers. The expansive white sand beaches are perfect for basking in the sun. It's renowned for its breathtaking sunsets and active nightlife, with numerous beachside bars and restaurants where you can enjoy local and international cuisine.
- **Mal País:** Mal País is cherished for its serene beaches and lush forests. Beyond relaxing in this tranquil environment, visitors can engage in adventure sports like zip-lining and ATV tours. The famous Cabo Blanco Nature Reserve also offers wildlife viewing and forest treks.
- **Jaco:** Jaco is not just a surfer's retreat but also the heart of Costa Rica's nightlife. During the day, visitors can enjoy horseback riding, deep-sea fishing, and exploring nearby national parks like Carrara. At night, Jaco comes alive with numerous bars, clubs, and live music venues.
- **Manuel Antonio:** This small area boasts one of the most visited conservations in Costa Rica, known for its beautiful beaches and rich biodiversity. Visitors can see wildlife, go parasailing, or simply relax on the beach, making it a perfect spot for adventure and relaxation.
- **Monteverde:** Monteverde is a unique area known for its cloud forests and incredible biodiversity. The Monteverde Cloud Forest Reserve attracts nature lovers and bird watchers seeking to glimpse the resplendent quetzal. The area offers numerous hiking trails and canopy tours.

Puntarenas will take you away from your hectic everyday life to a secluded, relaxing beach vacation. You will spend your days enjoying everything nature has to offer, from natural scenery to wildlife and beautiful beaches. You will go hiking, eat delicious food, and shop in unique local outlets.

Chapter 5: Alajuela

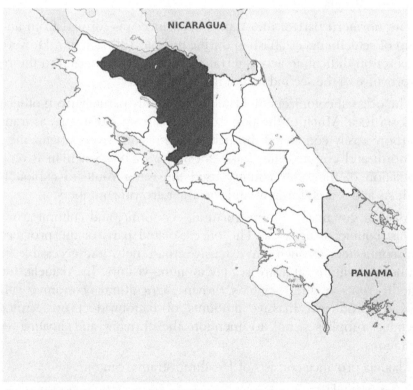

Breathtaking landscapes and cultural highlights make Alajuela a wonderful destination. *TUBS, CC BY-SA 4.0 <https://creativecommons.org/licenses/by-sa/4.0>, via Wikimedia Commons, https://commons.wikimedia.org/wiki/File:Costa_Rica,_administrative_divisions_-_de_-_monochrome.svg*

Continuing your journey through Costa Rica, this chapter explores Alajuela Province, its cantons, cultural highlights, breathtaking natural landscapes, and a broad range of landmarks and other attractions.

Historical and Background Information about Alajuela

Alajuela was founded by Catholic colonists, who were forced to find new settlements and parishes after the establishment of the city of Cartago in the late 16th century. As one of the new settlements, the role of the Alajuela parish was to help spread the religion to the population expanding westward. At the time of its establishment in the late 18th century, the settlement was known as La Lajuela and later became known as Villa Hermosa (which translates as the beautiful village), and eventually renamed Alajuela.

The northern part of the Alajuela province was formed from another group of settlements established during the late 19th century. However, as it was set on difficult-to-access terrain, it was only connected to the rest of the province in the second half of the 20th century.

The original colonizers of Alajuela came only partially from other parts of Costa Rica. Much of the population hails from Nicaragua, as transport was more easily conducted through the numerous rivers originating from the north and emptied into Lake Nicaragua or the San Juan River. The population of the latter country used the water route to exploit forest products and search for new lands for their growing numbers.

Alajuela saw massive infrastructural, economic, and cultural growth in the last couple of decades. The once isolated parts of the province are now connected through an extensive road network, accessible in all weather conditions, and are readily awaiting visitors. In Alajuela, tourists find the roots of the country's thriving agricultural economy, with the province producing massive amounts of nationwide crops, fruit, and vegetable supplies - not to mention the thriving and inviting coffee plantations.

Alajuela province consists of 16 administrative cantons:
- Alajuela
- Atenas
- Grecia
- Guatuso

- Los Chiles
- Naranjo
- Orotina
- Palmares
- Poás
- Río Cuarto
- San Carlos
- San Mateo
- San Ramón
- Sarchí
- Upala
- Zarcero

Did You Know?

For a few short years in the mid-1830s, Alajuela took over the role of Costa Rica's capital region before the title was transferred back to San Jose.

Main Attractions

Did You Know?

The Cultural Historical Museum of Alajuela and Costa Rica's main international airport are named after Juan Santamaría, a local soldier who showed incredible valor during the 1856 invasion by William Walker, the American military adventurer who wanted to conquer Costa Rica.

Cathedral of Alajuela

Cathedral of Alajuela.
Antonio Solera, CC BY 3.0 <https://creativecommons.org/licenses/by/3.0>, via Wikimedia Commons: https://commons.wikimedia.org/wiki/File:Alajuela,_Costa_Rica_-_Cathedral.png

Situated east of Parque Central, the monumental Cathedral of Alajuela is the highlight of Alajuela city. Erected in 1863, the cathedral embodies the perfect combination of religious influence and the era's architectural style. It boasts majestic gardens and invites visitors through its door, painted in a striking red. Inside it, you can see exceptional designs, adornments, and lots of colors.

As of the writing of this book, the regular opening hours are 6 am to 11:47 pm. However, please always double-check the opening hours online should there have been any slight change in their schedule.

Juan Santamaria Monument

Another attraction in Alajuela is the Juan Santamaria Monument, located in the city's Juan Santamaria Plaza. This unique bronze statue dedicated to the national hero Juan Santamaria is flanked by two cannons, showcasing his courage amid times of turmoil. The monuments were unveiled in mid-September 1891 as part of a celebration of those who gave their lives during the National Campaign against William Walker, enabling the country to maintain its independence.

La Fortuna

La Fortuna is home to the iconic Arenal Volcano.
Source: P. Hughes, CC BY-SA 4.0 <https://creativecommons.org/licenses/by-sa/4.0>, via Wikimedia Commons: https://commons.wikimedia.org/wiki/File:Costa_Rica_-_Arenal_volcano.jpg

The small but charming town of La Fortuna is home to the iconic Arenal Volcano, a must-see attraction for visitors in Costa Rica. Besides the unique sights it delivers, the area of the volcano offers much more than a place for pretty pictures and wonderment of nature. Here, you'll also find stunning waterfalls and hot springs to soak in, and if you're a true thrill seeker, you'll get your fill of adventures like whitewater rafting, rappelling, ziplining, hiking, and much more.

You can visit La Fortuna on any day, at any time.

San Ramón

San Ramón is often affectionately called the "City of Poets" due to its vibrant art scene and history. The town boasts several museums and natural habitats amid natural rainforest scenery, where, besides peeking into history, you can also embark on birdwatching adventures and experience Costa Rica's vast biodiversity up close. Museo de San Ramon is a gold museum under San Ramón's central plaza that is popular among tourists.

Grecia

Iglesia de Grecia.
The LEAF Project, CC BY-SA 2.0 <https://creativecommons.org/licenses/by-sa/2.0>, via Wikimedia Commons:
https://commons.wikimedia.org/wiki/File:Iglesia_de_La_Merced,_Grecia.jpg

Known for the striking gothic architecture of the Iglesia de Grecia (Metal Church) and the calm atmosphere of the Los Chorros Municipal Recreational Park, the village of Grecia offers tourists a relaxing environment for unlimited cultural exploration. It's away from the fast-paced life of the usual tourist hotspots, which makes it ideal for those looking to find some hidden gems amid the usual tourist hotspots. Grecia once boasted the title of the "cleanest town of Latin America," and for a good reason. The local farming community celebrates sustainable living and readily teaches visitors how to do the same.

Atenas

Like Grecia, Atenas is also known for its eco-friendly approach to living, which is why it has one of the best climates in the world, according to visitors. Whether you're looking to immerse yourself in the Costa Rican culture, for eternal spring-like weather for outdoor adventures, or a place to relax, you'll find it while exploring one of the town's landmarks, like the Parque Central.

Zarcero

Parroquia San Rafael Arcángel, Zarcero.

Sirujs Enobs, CC BY-SA 3.0 <https://creativecommons.org/licenses/by-sa/3.0>, via Wikimedia Commons: https://commons.wikimedia.org/wiki/File:Iglesia_de_San_Rafael,_Zarcero,_Costa_Rica_2004_-_panoramio.jpg

The town of Zarcero is celebrated for its whimsical topiary garden, which is made for picture taking and sitting in its central park. In contrast to the church across from it, the topiary boasts numerous figures of animals and objects shaped of ciprés, a type of coniferous plant showcasing a touch of local artisan culture. When you've finished admiring the topiary, make sure you look at the church as well, as it offers excellent insight into the local architectural history. Zarcero is surrounded by mountains and is set at a higher altitude than San Jose, which makes the temperatures in the area quite refreshing. It also provides opportunities to take in the picturesque mountain views.

Sarchí

Regarded as the cradle of Costa Rican craftsmanship, the look of Sarchí as it is known today was set in motion by an incredibly creative person working for the La Luisa coffee mill. It all started with one single colorful design painted on the wooden wheels and sides of an oxcart – for these to become the highlight of tourist attractions in the town. The production of these and similar artifacts, like intricate pieces of woodwork, is still popular, as the locals sell them as souvenirs (including a miniature version of the painted oxcarts). Visitors strolling on the main road through town can explore various workshops and stores and watch the local craftspeople create these traditional arts and handiworks. The church sitting at Sarchís center is also famous, primarily due to its unique pastel pink and green color combination, unlike similar monuments anywhere else. And, of course, you can't forget about the world's largest oxcart that put the town's name in the Guinness Book of World Records.

Transport

Despite being the country's third-largest province, Alajuela has many of its greatest attractions close together. You can travel through the province using taxis and Uber, with the former being more affordable and easy to find in the smaller towns. If you're staying in or near the major cities in this province, you can walk or rent a bike to get around, as the downtown area is typically connected to the main road. If you plan to cover larger distances or simply prefer to drive, you can rent a car or use the Costa Rican public transportation system. You'll find plenty of bus lines traveling to the nearby towns, with Station Wagon and TUASA covering the majority of the distance between the capital region and Alajuela. They also run several lines from Alajuela city to Poas, Sarchi, Heredia, San Ramon, and other nearby towns across the province.

Experiences

As small as it is, the General Tomas Guardia Park in Alajuela is just as inviting. It's one of the first places recommended to explore when you arrive in the city, as it helps you get a feel of the local culture. The park has an open space design, making it look larger than it is, yet it differentiates the space from the surrounding urban area. Walk around, sit on the stone benches flanked by palm trees, and watch the locals go about their days. There are often outdoor shows and live music playing, and if not, you can always admire the small fountain or purchase freshly made coconut drinks from nearby street vendors.

The General Tomas Guardia Park houses the Alajuela Cathedral and the Museo Histórico Cultural Juan Santamaría. Both are crucial historical architectural relics in Alajuela and probably the most easily accessible ones in the area. Touring the museum is free and can give visitors an insight into the county's rich history. The museum was once a barracks and prison building, playing a fundamental role in the Riva battle in 1856.

Besides historical artifacts like soldiers' uniforms and weaponry, the museum also features artworks illustrating numerous battles that shaped the country's history. There is also a children's activity area where your little ones can play history-based games and learn about important events in Costa Rican history.

Touring the world-renowned Poas Volcano is another highly recommended experience in Alajuela Province. With its mile-wide and thousand-foot-deep crater, the volcano is one of the world's largest open volcanoes. The breathtaking view from the crater rim makes it even more unique. You can easily reach the volcano area from Alajuela City Center, but you need to book your tour online in advance (tickets are also available at a nearby shop but are more expensive, and you may have to stand in line for a long time to get one). Visitors have a dedicated time slot for viewing, but you'll be thoroughly entertained while waiting your turn. Once you get the green light to go, you can awaken your inner adventurer and embark on a 1,640-foot hiking trail that culminates at the edge of the crater. Then, get your camera ready to start taking pictures, as you'll have about 20-30 minutes to do so before your time slot expires. If it is too cloudy for pictures, you can still enjoy the view in the cool, fresh area, as the temperatures at the volcano are always slightly lower than in the surrounding area.

If you want to make visiting the area an all-day program, you can book a guided tour of the Poas Volcano in the same package as you do a tour of La Paz Waterfall Gardens. This typically includes breakfast at Doka Coffee Estate, which you can also explore to your heart's content. At the La Paz Waterfall Gardens, feast your eyes on the enchanting scenery of natural surroundings, a hummingbird garden, and colorful butterflies native to this specific geographical topography.

If you're looking for a more culturally oriented experience, make sure you visit the Alajuela Municipal Theater. Bult in a classical neo-colonial style of 1950s Costa Rica, the theater is a historical architectural heritage site.

Hacienda Alsacia is another coffee lover's dream in Costa Rica. It embodies the mixture of traditional Costa Rican coffee making as it has a unique concept and belongs to the Starbucks franchise. Besides the coffee farm being open to the public, the property also serves as a research center, helping local farmers find sustainable ways to improve crop quality and profitability. Moreover, the stablemen promote tourism by inviting visitors to tours to learn about the coffee processing factory and the importance of good crop quality for making sustainable coffee products. Hacienda Alsacia is about 13 kilometers from Alajuela. It is recommended to book your tour in advance as this will grant you private parking (which you'll appreciate if using a rental car as parking in the area is notoriously challenging), a 90-minute informative tour, a souvenir, and, of course, the best part, which is the coffee tasting.

If you're in La Fortuna, you'll want to tour the Arenal Volcano, but make no mistake, this isn't the only experience you can have in this charming town. To get the most out of your visit to La Fortuna, book the Arenal Volcano Full-Day Combo Tour with Lunch and Dinner, and you'll have an unforgettable experience. The tour originally departs from San Jose, but you can request a pickup at your accommodation in Alajuela early in the morning. As your tour begins, you'll get to enjoy the scenic view of the mountains punctuated by volcanoes and coffee plantations on your drive to the first stop, La Casa del Café, where you can grab coffee and snacks. You'll then move on to the next landmark, La Paz Waterfall, and feast your eyes on the ancient rainforest encircling the world-famous waterfall. Next, you'll have an equally enchanting view of the San Fernando Waterfall, where you can take pictures of the natural beauty of the area, including the exotic birds native to the area. The tours also include a visit to the unique viewpoint bridge, from where you can observe the animals of the Iguanas Center habitat. The fun experiences continue with a visit to Adventure Arenal Park, where you can look at even more volcanoes and bask in the lush greenery of the rainforests. In case you get bored, you can also explore this veritable jungle by ziplining across it and the Arenal River and engage in the numerous entertainment efforts organized by the locals wanting to showcase their land's rich historical tapestry. Lastly, you can rest by soaking in one of the hot springs or refresh in the gushing waterfalls of the Hot Springs and Gardens, where you'll be surrounded by all the beauty you would expect from a tropical garden in Central America.

Where to Eat

One of the best eating experiences you'll have in Alajuela is at La Calle. This restaurant is set at the city's Plaza El Patio and offers the best of Costa Rican cuisine, along with excellent Sangria and local craft beers. On mild summer evenings, you can enjoy your meal in the restaurant's open-air seating area and embrace the vibe of the locals as they emerge from a long day of work.

Address: 100 meters north and 25 meters east of the Banco Nacional de la Tropicana, Plaza El Patio, Alajuela 20101, Costa Rica

In Fraijanes, near Poas Volcano, Freddo Fresas Restaurant is another option for sampling local cuisine.

Address: 5R43+VQJ, Provincia de Alajuela, Poás, Costa Rica

In comparison, MASQSABOR in Grecia offers a mixture of Latin and Mexican Dishes.

Address: C. 2 Lucas Fernández, Provincia de Alajuela, Grecia, Costa Rica (50 meters east of the Plaza, next door to the Post Office, Grecia 20301 Costa Rica)

Shopping Guide

Did You Know?

Alajuela is often dubbed the City of Mangoes due to its magnificent mango trees and the markets that are always flooded with fresh fruit and flowers. By buying these local products at the markets, you're learning about the local culture and supporting the local economy — not to mention brightening your day.

One of the best places to shop for locally sourced products is the Mercado Municipal de Alajuela, established in 1782. These are complex centralized markets where you can find fruit, vegetables, and other produce, small-scale traders, and numerous other local vendors offering products and services to both locals and tourists. Whether you're looking for coffee, meat, leather products, clothing, fish for your aquarium, jewelry, hammocks, or anything else, you'll be guaranteed to find them at Mercado Municipal de Alajuela. When you are tired of shopping, you can switch to sampling the best local cuisine at one of the city's cozy restaurants. The meals are made from traditional recipes with innovative twists to appeal to every taste. This colorful market, where you can have a unique look at a classic Central American market, is only one block away from General Tomas Guardia Park.

Entertainment

If you happen to visit Alajuela in January, head to Palmares, where you become part of the unique celebrations that mark the festival season. Known as Fiestas, the Palmares Festivities are one of the largest annual parties in the country, representing one of the best ways to immerse yourself in the local culture. Each year, hundreds of thousands of people participate in the Fiestas, including the parade called Tope, during which people cross the city on horseback. The celebrations also involve plenty of delicious Costa Rican delicacies and craft beer.

Sports and Leisure

If you're staying or visiting La Fortuna and love water adventures, you can take on canyoning, where, if you are brave enough, you can jump into one of the most stunning waterfalls you'll see while traveling on the rivers. An alternative option in La Fortuna and similar adventure-centered cities in the province is crossing a hanging bridge, which provides a unique view of the rainforests.

The Fraijanes Recreational Park near the Poás Volcano is another paradise for adventure seekers. It's particularly popular when the weather isn't ideal for hanging around the volcano itself, as you can hike on the winding trails a little further away. You can fish at the manmade lake in the park's center, birdwatch amid the trees, or have a picnic if you're looking for a more leisurely experience in the area.

Address: 4RF5+RHC, Alajuela Province, Sabanilla, Costa Rica

Accommodations

Did You Know?
Unlike San Jose, which lies a little over 19 kilometers southeast, Alajuela sits on a lower elevation, which gives it a slightly warmer climate. Due to the combination of this specific climate and high precipitation and humidity levels, the entire province seems like a tropical resort, wherever you happen to stay.

Another great thing about this province is that despite its spa-like surroundings, it can accommodate everyone's budget. Even if you are on a tight budget, you'll be able to find places in Alajuela that will feel like paradise and be affordable at the same time. Hotel Colinas del Sol in Atenas, for example, is a budget-friendly hotel with excellent views and amenities.

Address: C. Boquerón, Provincia de Alajuela, Atenas, Costa Rica

For those looking for a more luxurious experience, the province offers beautiful resort and spa hotels like the Vida Mountain Resort & Spa in San Ramon.

Address: 39QW+QWJ, Alajuela Province, San Ramon, Costa Rica

If you want to stay closer to one of the province's landmarks, you can find lodging at or near one of the striking coffee plantations and spend relaxing days away from the city's bustle and hustle. Some of the most recommended options are the budget-friendly Poas Lodge or Bosque de Paz.

Poas Lodge address: 5R6R+RFP, Varablanca Heredia CR, Heredia Province, 31698, Costa Rica

Bosque de Paz address: 14 kilometers northwest of Parque de Zarcero, Valle del Rio Toro, Alajuela, Alajuela, 21203, Costa Rica

Chapter 6: Guanacaste

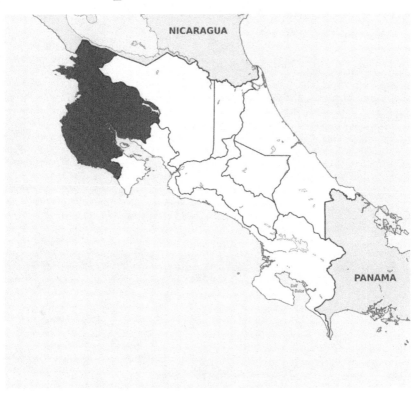

Guanacaste boasts prominent destinations and a vibrant local culture.
TUBS, CC BY-SA 4.0 <https://creativecommons.org/licenses/by-sa/4.0>, via Wikimedia Commons, https://commons.wikimedia.org/wiki/File:Costa_Rica_administrative_divisions_-_de_-_monochrome.svg

In this chapter, you'll discover the allure of Guanacaste, a province nestled in the northwest of Costa Rica celebrated for its breathtaking beaches, abundant biodiversity, and vibrant local culture. Guanacaste boasts prominent destinations, like the lively coastal town of Tamarindo, which is recognized for its top-notch surfing spots and lively nightlife. Immerse yourself in the natural wonders of Palo Verde National Park, where the Tempisque River winds its way through a surreal terrain of wetlands and dry forests, making it a haven for birdwatching enthusiasts.

Nature lovers will also find joy in exploring Rincon de la Vieja National Park, known for its volcanic landscapes, hot springs, and diverse wildlife. The provincial capital, Liberia, offers a unique blend of traditional Costa Rican charm and contemporary amenities, serving as a convenient gateway to the region's natural treasures. Whether you're seeking relaxation on pristine beaches, adventure in lush rainforests, or cultural experiences in charming towns, Guanacaste provides a diverse range of options for an unforgettable Costa Rican journey.

Historical and Background Information about Guanacaste

Guanacaste, located northwest of Costa Rica, has a rich history and a distinct cultural identity. Originally inhabited by indigenous Chorotega communities, the region witnessed Spanish colonization in the 16th century. The Spanish influence left a lasting mark on Guanacaste, evident in its architecture, traditions, and language. The province became a part of Nicaragua in the early 19th century but later joined Costa Rica in 1825. Guanacaste's decision to join Costa Rica resulted from a referendum where the population expressed a strong desire to be part of the emerging nation.

This historical event is commemorated annually on July 25th, known as the "Guanacaste Day," celebrating the province's annexation to Costa Rica. Over the years, Guanacaste has evolved into a key economic and tourism hub, renowned for its beautiful beaches, national parks, and vibrant cultural heritage. Today, the province is a testament to its diverse past, offering visitors a blend of historical charm and natural beauty.

Main Attractions of Guanacaste

Tamarindo Beach

Tamarindo Beach.
Jarle Naustvik, CC BY 2.0 <https://creativecommons.org/licenses/by/2.0>, via Wikimedia Commons: https://commons.wikimedia.org/wiki/File:Tamarindo_beach-Guanacaste-Costa_Rica.jpg

Tamarindo Beach, situated on the Pacific coast, is a magnetic destination for surf enthusiasts, offering consistent waves for all skill levels. The town itself is a vibrant mix of laid-back charm and lively energy, with an array of beachfront bars, restaurants, and shops. The beach is a haven for surfers and a perfect spot for sunbathing and enjoying spectacular Pacific sunsets. The warm waters of Tamarindo attract diverse marine life, making them ideal for snorkeling and boat tours.

Did You Know?

Tamarindo was a quiet fishing village that transformed into a bustling tourist destination. However, efforts have been made to maintain its ecological balance and protect the nesting sea turtles.

Palo Verde National Park

Palo Verde National Park.
Debivort at the English Wikipedia, GFDL <http://www.gnu.org/copyleft/fdl.html>, via Wikimedia Commons: https://commons.wikimedia.org/wiki/File:PaloVerdeRocaview.jpg

Palo Verde National Park is a wetland and dry forest ecosystem centered on the Tempisque River. Guided boat tours offer an immersive experience, allowing visitors to observe crocodiles, monkeys, iguanas, and a myriad of bird species, including herons and storks. The park's conservation efforts contribute significantly to the protection of Costa Rica's rich biodiversity.

Opening Hours:
- Every day from 8 am to 4 pm.

As of the writing of this book, the aforementioned are the regular opening hours. However, please always double-check the opening hours online should there have been any slight change in their schedule.

Did You Know?

Palo Verde is designated a Ramsar Site, recognizing its international importance as a wetland ecosystem.

Rincón de la Vieja National Park

Rincón de la Vieja hot spring.
user:Flicka, CC BY-SA 3.0 <http://creativecommons.org/licenses/by-sa/3.0/>, via Wikimedia Commons: https://commons.wikimedia.org/wiki/File:Rinc%C3%B3n_de_la_Vieja_Hot_Spring.jpg

This national park is a volcanic wonderland featuring the active Rincón de la Vieja Volcano. Trails lead to bubbling mud pots, hot springs, and waterfalls, providing visitors with an adventurous hiking experience. The park's diverse landscapes include tropical forests inhabited by howler monkeys and tapirs, creating a haven for nature lovers.

Opening Hours:
- Tuesday to Sunday from 8 AM to 3:30 PM.
- Closed on Monday.

As of the writing of this book, the aforementioned are the regular opening hours. However, please always double-check the opening hours online should there have been any slight change in their schedule.

Did You Know?

The folklore surrounding Rincon de la Vieja tells of a local legend about a young girl, Princess Curubanda, who fell in love with the head of a rival tribe and was thrown into the volcano by her father. She lived on the other side of the volcano as a recluse and became a shaman. Rincon de la Vieja means "corner of the old woman" in honor of the princess.

Liberia

Liberia, the provincial capital, offers a mix of historic charm and modern amenities. Its colonial-style architecture, seen in structures like the

Church of La Ermita and the Guanacaste Museum, provides a glimpse into the area's rich history. The bustling markets and local eateries showcase the town's cultural vibrancy. Liberia serves as a convenient gateway to the region's natural wonders.

Did You Know?

Liberia is often called "La Ciudad Blanca" due to the prevalence of white adobe structures and the white gravel that once made the city's roads, and it serves as a hub for those venturing into the nearby national parks.

Guanacaste Conservation Area

This extensive conservation area encompasses several national parks, including Santa Rosa, Guanacaste, and Rincón de la Vieja. The parks protect diverse ecosystems, from dry forests to cloud forests, and are vital to preserving the region's unique flora and fauna.

Did You Know?

The Guanacaste Conservation Area connects different ecosystems, facilitating wildlife movement and contributing to genetic diversity.

Playa Conchal

Playa Conchal.
El Pantera, CC BY-SA 4.0 <https://creativecommons.org/licenses/by-sa/4.0>, via Wikimedia Commons: https://commons.wikimedia.org/wiki/File:Playa_El_Conchal_-_IMG_20230430_172417.jpg

Playa Conchal is renowned for its unusual sandy shores made up of crushed seashells. The crystal-clear waters and coral reefs make it an ideal spot for snorkeling. The nearby Conchal Reserve offers opportunities for nature walks, allowing visitors to witness the beauty of the tropical dry forest.

You can visit Playa Conchal any day and at any time during your trip.

Did You Know?

The unique sand of Playa Conchal results from the constant erosion and breaking down of shells by the ocean, creating a beach with a distinct texture and appearance.

Transportation in Guanacaste

Daniel Oduber Quirós International Airport

The main gateway to Guanacaste, Daniel Oduber Quirós International Airport in Liberia, provides convenient access to the region. It facilitates domestic and international flights.

Road Networks

Guanacaste is well-connected by a network of roads accessible by car or bus. The Pan-American Highway runs through the province, directly linking to major cities and attractions. Renting a car offers flexibility in exploring the diverse landscapes at your own pace.

Public Buses

The public bus system is an affordable and environmentally friendly option for travel within Guanacaste. However, schedules may vary, and travel times can be longer than private transportation.

Taxis and Ridesharing

Taxis are readily available in urban areas and can be hailed on the streets or booked through mobile apps. You can also look into ridesharing services; these are becoming more prevalent, convenient, and reliable.

Car Rentals

Renting a car is a popular choice for exploring Guanacaste independently. Several international and local car rental agencies operate in the region, offering a range of vehicles. This option provides the flexibility to visit remote areas and access off-the-beaten-path destinations.

Domestic Flights

For travelers looking to save time, domestic flights are available from Daniel Oduber Quirós International Airport to other airports within Costa Rica. This option is handy for reaching more remote destinations or connecting to other regions of the country.

Did You Know?

Guanacaste's roadways offer picturesque journeys through diverse landscapes, from coastal panoramas to mountainous terrain. While driving, keep an eye out for the iconic "Guanacaste" trees lining the roads, adding to the region's natural beauty. Additionally, road trips provide opportunities to discover hidden gems, such as local roadside eateries offering authentic Costa Rican cuisine and glimpses into the daily life of the province.

Experiences in Guanacaste

Surfing Adventures in Tamarindo

Tamarindo is a haven for surf enthusiasts of all levels. Whether you're a seasoned surfer or a beginner, local surf schools offer lessons to help you catch the perfect wave. The laid-back atmosphere and consistent waves make for a memorable surfing experience.

Wildlife Safaris in Palo Verde National Park

Embark on a wildlife safari along the Tempisque River in Palo Verde National Park. Guided boat tours provide an up-close encounter with crocodiles, monkeys, and many bird species. It's a nature lover's paradise, offering a unique perspective on Costa Rica's diverse ecosystems.

Hiking and Hot Springs at Rincon de la Vieja

Explore the volcanic landscapes of Rincon de la Vieja National Park through well-maintained hiking trails. Witness bubbling mud pots and sparkling waterfalls, and rejuvenate in natural hot springs. The park's diverse terrain ensures an adventurous and immersive experience.

Cultural Discovery in Liberia

Immerse yourself in the cultural heritage of Liberia by exploring its historic architecture, vibrant markets, and local eateries. The Guanacaste Museum provides insights into the region's history. Attend local events or festivals to experience the lively traditions and warm hospitality of the Guanacaste people.

Ziplining and Canopy Tours

For adrenaline-seekers, Guanacaste offers thrilling ziplining and canopy tours. Soar through the treetops, experiencing the region's lush landscapes from a different perspective. Several eco-adventure parks provide a perfect blend of excitement and nature appreciation.

Beach Bliss at Playa Conchal

Indulge in the pristine beauty of Playa Conchal, known for its unique crushed shell sand. Relax on the beach, snorkel in the crystal-clear waters, or explore the nearby Conchal Reserve for nature walks. It's a perfect spot for unwinding and enjoying the natural splendor of Guanacaste.

Did You Know?

Guanacaste hosts the "Fiestas Civicas," a series of civic festivals celebrating the annexation of the province to Costa Rica. These festivities, around July 25th, include parades, traditional dances, rodeos, and bullfights. Attending these events provides a firsthand experience of the local culture and the province's historical significance. Additionally, watch for "sabaneros," the traditional Costa Rican northern cowboys, showcasing their horsemanship skills during these celebrations.

Family Fun in Guanacaste

Diamante Eco Adventure Park

Diamante Eco Adventure Park is an excellent family destination featuring a wildlife sanctuary, ziplining, and an animal and reptile exhibition. The park's dual zipline, one of the longest in Central America, provides a thrilling experience for older kids and adults, making it an exciting day out for the whole family.

Address: RIU Hotel 350 east, Provincia de Guanacaste, Playa Matapalo, 50503, Costa Rica

Ostional Wildlife Refuge - Turtle Watching

Take the family to witness the extraordinary phenomenon of turtle nesting at the Ostional Wildlife Refuge. Depending on the time of year, you may have the chance to see Olive Ridley sea turtles laying their eggs or witness baby turtles hatching. It's a unique and educational experience for all ages.

Address: X8Q2+XQ8, Guanacaste Province, Ostional, Costa Rica

Playa Flamingo - Family-Friendly Beach Days

Playa Flamingo offers a family-friendly beach setting with calm waters and golden sands. Enjoy a day of building sandcastles, swimming, and beachcombing. Water activities like paddleboarding and snorkeling are also available for older kids and teens, which is super for a family beach day!

Llanos de Cortez Waterfall Excursion

A short drive from Liberia, the Llanos de Cortez waterfall provides a refreshing natural playground for the whole family. Enjoy picnics by the waterfall, swim in its cool pool, and explore the surrounding lush scenery. The relatively easy hike is a family-friendly outdoor adventure suitable for children.

Monkey Park - Monkey Sanctuary

Monkey Park near Tamarindo offers an educational and entertaining experience for families. In a natural environment, encounter various monkey species, including capuchins and howlers. The park also features other wildlife, creating a fun and informative outing for kids. It's an opportunity for families to connect with Costa Rica's rich biodiversity.

Where to Eat

Nogui's Restaurant (Tamarindo)

A beachfront gem in Tamarindo, Nogui's offers a diverse menu featuring fresh seafood, Costa Rican specialties, and international dishes. The relaxed atmosphere and ocean views make it a favorite for both locals and tourists.

Address: 75X4+9W7, 155, Provincia de Guanacaste, Tamarindo, Costa Rica

El Viejo Oeste (Santa Cruz)

Experience a taste of local Guanacaste flavors at El Viejo Oeste. Known for its traditional Costa Rican dishes, the restaurant offers a cozy ambiance and a chance to savor authentic regional cuisine in the heart of Santa Cruz.

Seasons by Shlomy (Tamarindo)

Seasons by Shlomy is a fine-dining restaurant with a diverse menu that includes fresh seafood, steaks, and Mediterranean-inspired dishes. The elegant setting is perfect for a unique dining experience.

Adress: Central Ave 500, Guanacaste Province, Tamarindo, Costa Rica

Café Liberia (Liberia)

Café Liberia in Liberia is a popular choice for a taste of local Tico cuisine. This family-friendly restaurant serves hearty portions of Costa Rican comfort food, including casados and gallo pinto.

Address: Calle Real, 150 M. South From Tienda la Nueva Casa Zuniga-Chlachar Liberia - Guanacaste - Costa Rica, Liberia 50101 Costa Rica

Lolas (Playa Avellana)

Lolas, situated in Playa Avellana, fuses international and Costa Rican flavors, and its menu caters to various dietary preferences. Lolas is known for its creative dishes and vibrant atmosphere.

Address: Playa Avellana, Beach front Provincia de Guanacaste Playa Avellana, 50303, Costa Rica

Soda La Teresita (Coco)

For an authentic Costa Rican "soda" experience, visit Soda La Teresita in Nicoya. This casual eatery serves home-style dishes, including delicious casados and other local specialties, providing an affordable and tasty dining option.

Address: H822+JQC, Ruta Nacional Secundaria 151, Provincia de Guanacaste, Coco, Costa Rica

Did You Know?

Costa Rican cuisine often includes "casados," a traditional meal consisting of rice, black beans, plantains, salad, and a choice of protein such as fish, chicken, or beef. Each restaurant puts its own unique twist on this classic dish, making it a must-try during your culinary exploration of Guanacaste.

Shopping Guide in Guanacaste

Guanacaste Souvenirs

When in Guanacaste, explore local markets and souvenir shops for unique items that capture the essence of the region. Look for handmade crafts, pottery, traditional textiles, and wood carvings that reflect the rich cultural heritage of Guanacaste.

Nicoya Market (Nicoya)

Nicoya, the historic city, is home to a bustling market where you can find a variety of local products. From fresh produce to handmade crafts, this market offers a glimpse into daily life in Guanacaste. Don't miss the chance to pick up authentic Costa Rican coffee and spices.

Address: 4GRX+FH8, C. 5, Provincia de Guanacaste, Nicoya, Costa Rica

Tamarindo Farmer's Market (Tamarindo)

Tamarindo's Farmer's Market is a vibrant spot where local artists showcase their talents. Browse through stalls featuring handmade jewelry, artwork, and clothing. It's an excellent place to find unique souvenirs and support the local arts scene.

Address: 75X5+6RH, 152, Provincia de Guanacaste, Tamarindo, Costa Rica

Liberia Central Market (Liberia)

The Liberia Central Market is a cultural hub where you can discover the local atmosphere and stalls selling traditional Costa Rican goods, including coffee, spices, and handmade crafts. It's a great place to interact with locals and discover authentic products.

Playa Flamingo Flea Market (Playa Flamingo)

If you're in Playa Flamingo, check out the local flea market for a mix of handmade crafts, clothing, and beachwear. The market often features local artisans, providing an opportunity to purchase one-of-a-kind items and support the community.

Entertainment in Guanacaste

Papagayo Gulf Sunset Cruise (Playa del Coco)

Experience the magic of a Papagayo Gulf Sunset Cruise departing from Playa del Coco. Sail along the scenic coastline, enjoy live music, and witness a breathtaking sunset over the Pacific. Some cruises include dinner and entertainment for a memorable evening on the water.

Coco Beach Casino (Playa del Coco)

For those seeking a bit of nightlife and entertainment, the Coco Beach Casino in Playa del Coco offers gaming excitement. Test your luck at the slot machines or try your hand at various table games. The casino often hosts events and live entertainment.

Congo Trail Canopy Tour (Liberia)

For an adventurous and entertaining experience, consider the Congo Trail Canopy Tour in Liberia. Zip through the treetops on exhilarating zip lines, providing an adrenaline rush and stunning views of the surrounding landscapes.

Flamingo Beach Resort and Spa (Playa Flamingo)

Some resorts in Playa Flamingo, such as the Flamingo Beach Resort and Spa, offer evening entertainment options. Enjoy live music, themed dinners, and cultural shows organized by the resort. It's a chance to unwind and be entertained without leaving the comfort of your accommodation.

Nightlife in Tamarindo

Tamarindo boasts a lively nightlife scene with beachfront bars, clubs, and live music venues. Explore spots like Crazy Monkey Bar or Pangas Beach Club for a mix of local vibes and international beats. It's the perfect way to wrap up a day of exploring the region.

Did You Know?

Guanacaste's nightlife often revolves around beachside gatherings and live music. Many beach towns, including Tamarindo and Playa Flamingo, feature open-air venues where visitors can enjoy the cool ocean breeze while listening to local bands or international DJs. The combination of music, ocean views, and a vibrant atmosphere is unique and enjoyable entertainment in the province.

Accommodation in Guanacaste

Westin Reserva Conchal (Playa Conchal)

Right off Playa Conchal, The Westin Reserva Conchal offers a luxurious stay with a golf course, spa, and spacious suites. The resort's all-inclusive options provide a hassle-free experience, and its beachfront location offers stunning views and direct access to one of Costa Rica's most beautiful beaches.

Address: Playa Conchal Guanacaste, Guanacaste Province, 50308, Costa Rica

Margaritaville Beach Resort (Playa Flamingo)

Margaritaville Beach Resort in Playa Flamingo is a tropical paradise offering comfortable accommodations with a touch of Caribbean flair.

Enjoy ocean-view rooms, multiple dining options, and amenities like a spa and infinity pool. The resort's vibrant atmosphere captures the essence of a laid-back beach lifestyle.

Address: Guanacaste Province, Playa Flamingo, 50308, Costa Rica

Andaz Costa Rica Resort at Peninsula Papagayo (Papagayo Peninsula)

Situated on the exclusive Papagayo Peninsula, the Andaz Costa Rica Resort blends luxury and natural beauty. Surrounded by a rainforest, the resort features modern design, upscale dining, and stunning views of the Pacific Ocean.

Address: Peninsula Papagayo, Guanacaste Province, Papagayo Peninsula, 50104, Costa Rica

Casa Chameleon Hotel (Las Catalinas)

Casa Chameleon Hotel at Las Catalinas provides private villas with breathtaking ocean views for a romantic and secluded getaway. The infinity pool, gourmet dining, and personalized service are perfect for couples seeking a tranquil escape on the Nicoya Peninsula.

Address: Playa Danta, Potrero, Provincia de Guanacaste, Las Catalinas, Costa Rica

Hotel Punta Islita, Autograph Collection (Punta Islita)

Located in a secluded cove, Hotel Punta Islita offers an upscale experience with oceanfront villas surrounded by tropical gardens. The resort emphasizes sustainability and cultural authenticity, giving its guests a unique and immersive Costa Rican experience.

Address: 160, Guanacaste Province, Punta Islita, 50201, Costa Rica

JW Marriott Guanacaste Resort & Spa (Hacienda Pinilla)

Set within the Hacienda Pinilla community, JW Marriott Guanacaste Resort & Spa combines opulence with local charm. Guests can enjoy elegant rooms, a championship golf course, a spa, and multiple dining options. The resort's hacienda-style architecture reflects the cultural richness of Guanacaste.

Address: Hacienda Pinilla, Provincia de Guanacaste, Guanacaste, 50309, Costa Rica

Did You Know?

Many accommodations in Guanacaste embrace sustainable and eco-friendly practices, aiming to minimize their environmental impact. From eco-lodges to upscale resorts, several regional establishments participate in conservation efforts, such as waste reduction, energy efficiency, and support for local community initiatives. When choosing accommodation, consider places that prioritize responsible tourism to contribute to the preservation of Guanacaste's natural beauty.

Chapter 7: Cartago and Heredia

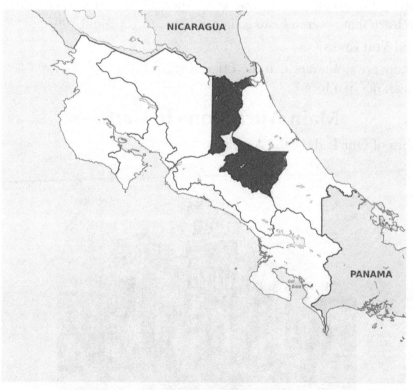

The gems of Costa Rica.
TUBS, CC BY-SA 4.0 <https://creativecommons.org/licenses/by-sa/4.0>, via Wikimedia Commons, https://commons.wikimedia.org/wiki/File:Costa_Rica_administrative_divisions_-_de_-_monochrome.svg

Cartago and Heredia are two of the many gems in Costa Rica. They are renowned for their warm, welcoming culture, historical sights, and natural splendor. For these reasons, tourists are sure to make a pit stop in these cities to enjoy all the wonder they offer.

Historical and Background Information about Cartago

The city of Cartago is located in the east-central fertile valley of Costa Rica, standing at 4720 feet above sea level, right at the foot of Irazu Volcano. The foundation of the city was laid in 1563 by Juan Vasquez de Coronado, and it remained the country's central city for 260 years until 1823. Due to its close proximity to the volcano, the city was subjected to repeated earthquakes and volcanic eruptions that left no colonial buildings standing. One such disaster was an earthquake in 1910 and an eruption from Irazu that covered Cortago in ash between 1963 and 1965.

Did You Know?

Many are not aware that the original capital of Costa Rica was actually Cartago, not San Jose.

Main Attractions in Cartago

Basilica of Our Lady of the Angels

Basilica of Our Lady of the Angels.
Mariordo (Mario Roberto Durán Ortiz), CC BY-SA 4.0 <https://creativecommons.org/licenses/by-sa/4.0>, via Wikimedia Commons:
https://commons.wikimedia.org/wiki/File:Basilica_Virgen_de_los_Angeles_CRI_07_2018_0319.jpg

The Basilica of the Patroness of Costa Rica is one of the most visited destinations in Cartago.

As legend would have it, the story started when a young girl happened upon a small statue of the Virgin Mary holding baby Jesus on a rock. She took the statue home with her, only to wake up the following day to find it had disappeared from her room. Upon further investigation, it was found back at its original location, on the same rock she had found it on the previous day. The girl then decided to take the small statue to the local priest, who locked it up in a small box for the night. In the morning, the statue was once again found on the rock. The little statue is often referred to as "La Negrita" (or "the Dear Black one") in reference to its color.

Initially, the Basilica was built in a different location but was repeatedly damaged by earthquakes. Some believed this was a sign from the Virgin to build it in the original place where the statue was found. It was decided to move the building to where the statue was first found in 1635. The building is a unique mixture of Colonial and Byzantine cultures.

The site is most crowded in the days leading up to August 2nd due to the long-lasting Costa Rican tradition called the Romeria. The Romeria is a pilgrimage that millions of devout believers from San Jose and other cities undertake. The walk is about 22 kilometers, and some worshippers choose to crawl on their hands and knees for part of the journey as a sign of their devotion.

Opening Hours:
- Every day from 6 AM to 7 PM.

As of the writing of this book, the aforementioned are the regular opening hours. However, please always double-check the opening hours online should there have been any slight change in their schedule.

Did You Know?

The pilgrims often bring along small silver medals representing different body parts they are concerned about. The little tokens are left in front of the statue in the hope that her blessings will cure them. In the Basilica, the visitors bathed and drank water from the rock where the statue was found.

You can probably tour the Basilica in an hour. The site has a serene and quiet nature where you can sit in silence and enjoy the atmosphere. Within walking distance of La Negrita, there are several facilities and places to rest and eat after a long walk.

The Ruins of Santiago Apóstol Parish

The Ruins of Santiago Apóstol Parish.
Daniel32708 - Daniel Vargas, CC BY-SA 3.0 <https://creativecommons.org/licenses/by-sa/3.0>, via Wikimedia Commons: https://commons.wikimedia.org/wiki/File:Old-ruins-in-cartago-daniel-vargas19.jpg

The ruins of Cartago are among some of the favorite destinations for adventure seekers. The beautiful parish, whose construction was interrupted on March 4th of 1910 as a result of the Santa Monica earthquake, stands proudly in front of the Plaza Mayor square.

The Santiago Apostol Parish ruins offer a magnificent mix of natural beauty and cultural heritage. A stunning tropical garden grew among the fallen walls of the site and gray blocks that make a beautiful and relaxing walk, especially if you arrive in the early morning.

The ruins of Cartago carry with them the story of the local's resilience and devotion to build, repair, and rebuild the fallen churches. The site is home to several churches rather than just one. The most ancient of them was built in the 1600s and later destroyed in 1630 by an earthquake, a recurring natural disaster in the country due to its volcanic nature.

The first consecrated church in 1662 was destroyed three times by three different earthquakes. Every time the tragedy hit, the locals would rise to mend the damage until 1841, when the San Antolin earthquake struck. At the start of the 1900s, devout worshippers and parishioners attempted for the final time to rebuild the church until the earthquake in Santa Monica had another say in the matter.

By then, the locals had adopted the belief that the ruins were actually cursed and that it was better to let them be.

Opening Hours:
- Every day from 7 AM to 4:30 PM

As of the writing of this book, the aforementioned are the regular opening hours. However, please always double-check the opening hours online should there have been any slight change in their schedule.

Did You Know?

There is a story tied to the curse. It was said that once upon a time, there were two brothers; a priest and a single, pleasant young man. One day, they both fell in love with the same woman, and a rivalry began when she didn't choose the priest. In 1577, the animosity reached its boiling point when the priest killed his brother at the New Year's Mass. To pay penance for his crime, the priest built a church, which was destroyed a year later. Every time anyone attempted to rebuild it, an earthquake would hit it and tear it down. Legend has it that to this day, in the fog, you can see the priest wandering in the ruins headless, paying for his sin for all eternity.

The ruins are easily reached with a half-hour drive to the southeast of San Jose. They are located right at the center of Cartago City.

The ruins are open from 7:00 am to 4:30 pm, except on holidays. It is wise to check the local website before visiting to avoid missing out.

Restaurants surround the attraction, within walking distance from the Basilica.

Orosi

The valley of Orosi is well known for its peaceful nature, towering pine trees, and tranquil river. It's also known to be home to some of the best coffee in the world. If you are looking for an escape from the city lights and a reconnecting with Mother Nature, this trip is for you.

The area is home to national parks, thermal spas, and museums. You can book horseback riding tours, go bird watching, visit local farms, taste delicious coffee, and go on long hikes through the greenery. You can even visit the famous Irazu Volcano while there.

Main Attractions in Orosi

While in the area, you can visit the Iglesia de San José De Orosi, one of the oldest churches in the country, surrounded by a beautiful flower garden. Its design represents Spanish colonial architecture. The church also has a tiny museum attached, displaying interesting artifacts from the culture.

Iglesia de San José De Orosi.
David Broad, CC BY 3.0 <https://creativecommons.org/licenses/by/3.0>, via Wikimedia Commons: https://commons.wikimedia.org/wiki/File:Iglesia_de_San_Jose_de_Orosi_-_Costa_Rica_-_panoramio_(4).jpg

You should also consider visiting the Ruins of Ujarras, built in 1693. These ruins are a testament to how the original settlers in Costa Rica went about their lives.

Sports and Leisure in Orosi

If you're into nature, you can book a trip to the Cachi Dam or the Presa de Cachi. You can go on the Reventazon River for a rafting adventure. There is also the option to zip line through the forest and sugar cane fields. In the south, there is the Tapanti National Park, known for being the place of discovery of 3 different Orchid species.

The small valley is about 40 kilometers away from San Jose. The bus ride from Cartago to Orosi can take around 20 minutes. If you are still in the planning phase of your trip, check the transportation schedules and pick the exact destination where you want to be dropped off. Orosi Volcano is not the same as Orosi Station. One is 5 hours away, while the other is 20 minutes away, so be careful when booking your travel schedule.

Turrialba

Turrialba is an area surrounded by rivers and mountains, a perfect destination for adventure seekers and people who appreciate nature and a good adrenaline rush.

Located east of Cartago, the trip from Cartago to Turrialba takes 30 minutes by bus, the cheapest means of transportation. The next cheapest is a car ride; the most expensive is to go by taxi. The weather is cool. However, it is a little bit more humid than Cartago due to its close proximity to the Caribbean. The ideal time to visit would probably be between November and April, during the dry season.

The volcanic mountain valley is about 29 kilometers away from Cartago. The area has indigenous sites, national parks, and archeological monuments. It is a haven for birdwatchers, given that 150 different species of birds are attracted to its forests and water bodies. Adventure seekers can either go whitewater rafting or kayaking on one of its rivers or hike up the Turrialba Volcano, which is 10,958 feet above sea level. The hike, though, is at your own risk, given that this is one of the most active volcanoes in all of Costa Rica.

One of the main attractions is located 19 kilometers north of Turrialba. This is the Guayabo National Monument. The story goes that in ancient times, the hunters used the rivers nearby for hunting, catching their prey when the animals stopped to drink water.

Did You Know?

This is one of the only monuments discovered depicting the pre-Columbian era. The site gives valuable insight into what life might have been like between 1000 BC and 1400 AD.

Transport in Cartago

If you plan to stay in Cartago for a while, it is wise to use one of the sightseeing tour buses to explore the city. The option doesn't just include exploration but also an array of other services, including hotel accommodations and airport pickups and drop-offs. These buses also offer discounts for small children and the elderly.

Cartago is not the easiest city in which to rent a car. However, it is close enough to San Jose, where the feat is a little bit easier. With this option, you'll be able to move around the provinces at your own pace and take your time sightseeing, whether visiting the Irazu Volcano, Turrialba, or any other provinces nearby.

Entertainment

While in the city, consider visiting the Anfiteatro Municipal de Cartago. The theater is known to be the home of many different performing arts, including dance shows, circus, and music festivals.

Where to Eat

There is a wide array of restaurants in Cartago. If you're looking for budget-friendly local cuisine, visit Bacadito Del Cielo, La Posada de la Luna, or Mi Tierra. These restaurants offer breakfast, lunch, and dinner at a reasonable price.

Accommodations

The hotels and accommodations in Cartago are known for their welcoming staff. Among the top-rated hotels are Hotel Quelitales, where you will be treated to a wonderful view of nature, Casa Mora B&B, which is close to the Basilica de Los Angeles, and Grandpas Hotel.

Shopping Guide

Try visiting the Cartago Central Market in the city (Mercado Central). The market is where the locals shop and is quite close to the Basilica of Our Lady of Los Angeles. It has all kinds of stalls that serve local cuisine. Even though it can be crowded, the area is well-organized and clean.

If you're looking for a more urban experience, you can visit the Paseo Metropoli, a shopping mall that lies within 9.5 kilometers of the ruins of Carthage.

Historical Background and Information about Heredia

Heredia, also known as the City of Flowers, began its construction in the year 1706. The city sits in the center of Costa Rica, surrounded by coffee plantations and forests. Heredia is well known for its colonial construction that litters the entire city.

Did You Know?

The City of Flowers earned its name from the abundance of floral and green areas present in the city.

Main Attractions

One of the sites that usually teems with visitors is the La Inmaculada, an ancient church that was started to being built in 1797.

The church is situated in the central park and surrounded by many restaurants and local shops.

Experiences

While in Parque Central, you can also spend some time in the music temple, 'which is also where you can find El Fortin. El Fortin is an old colonial tower that still stands as an original colonial art expression.

El Fortin was built in 1876 by the governor Fadrique Gutierrez Guardia. Initially, the plan was to build four of the same structures around the city. However, only one was constructed. The small holes in the tower make for excellent sniper stations to protect the city.

As of the writing of this book, opening hours for El Fortin are 8 am to 4 pm. However, we highly advise that you double-check these times.

Another reason that the city is quite popular is because it houses the most prominent university in Costa Rica, Universidad Nacional. The National University has one of the top biological and environmental schools. The school includes one of Central America's principal veterinarian schools and an incredible marine biology section.

Barva

An escape not too far away from Heredia, Barva is a beautiful, culturally rich area between the mountains of extinct volcanoes. The little town is only 10 minutes away from Heredia. At Barva, you'll have the unique experience of tasting locally sourced coffee from local beans. The coffee is nurtured and grown on the slopes of the hills.

The name Barva comes from Barvac, which is what the last local pre-colonial Indian chief was called. The locals will take you down memory lane, explaining the culture of the area and how the chief impacted the birth of the town before Spanish colonialism.

The volcanic nature of the soil makes it a perfect land to grow local crops and lush greenery. If you're a nature lover, you'll find that the area attracts all kinds of critters and fauna. You can arrange the coffee tours with the locals or the staff at the hotel. Nature lovers will be pleased to hear that this is the area where Barva volcano exists. The volcano lies northeast of San Jose.

Did You Know?

The peak of the Barva volcano is considered one of three mountain tops to make up the "Las Tres" Mountains. The volcano is also considered the third highest in the country, following Irazu and Turrialba.

It is believed that the last time the mountain erupted was in the 1700s.

The location is known for being a natural escape from the hustle and bustle of the city and a beautiful escape for those interested in bird watching or going on long hikes in the mountains.

Sarapiqui

The town of Puerto Viejo de Sarapiquí lies to the northeast of the country. It is about 85 kilometers from the capital of San Jose. Sarapiqui is known as a favorite travel destination for adventure seekers and has an unmatched biodiversity. It is one of the few places where the Green Macaw still exists. The little town is known for having several natural parks and reserves that protect wildlife.

For someone looking to immerse themselves in the culture and get to know the locals, the town is known for its colorful festivities like bull riding, cattle shows, and outdoor fairs.

Sarapiqui is one of the many areas in Costa Rica that cultivate and produce coffee. However, that is not all. They are also famous for planting bananas, cardamom, cacao, and many other plants and fruits.

The flow of the river Rio Sarapiqui is one of the reasons the area is fertile, not to mention the balanced climate is known to be moderate throughout the seasons.

Experiences

Suppose you happen to find yourself in Sarapiqui. In that case, you must add the International La Selva Biological Research Station to your itinerary! The area houses the most diverse collection of plants, greenery, and wildlife animals. It includes ample opportunities for white water rafting, hiking, and nature walks. You can also take a boat down the river to try and catch glimpses of caimans, birds, and turtles. For avian enthusiasts, you can see hummingbirds, dippers, guans, agoutis, and many other bird species.

La Selva is not the only wildlife park there; there is also Braulio Carrillo National Park. The 108K acres of forest houses the Barva Volcano. It has over 150 animal species and 500 birds!

Santo Domingo

Santo Domingo is yet another one of the beautiful colonial towns of Costa Rica that happens to be surrounded by lush and magnificent landscapes. It only takes a few minutes to get there from the south of Heredia. The small town is quiet and serene, giving you a golden opportunity to explore all the nature that Costa Rica has to offer. If you're looking to keep away from the crowded life of San Jose, this city is an ideal destination, and it is not far away or hard to get to.

The architecture is unique in its Spanish colonial features. The old churches depict clear examples of what 19th-century buildings looked like. As you walk down the streets, it will feel like you're being transported through time and experiencing the days of the birth of Costa Rica.

One of the most admired buildings is the church of Santo Domingo de Guzman Basilica. The white church stands guard over the city with its towers covered with golden domes.

After you've soaked in all the architectural beauty, it will be time to head out to the INBioparque or INBio Park. The mission for the National Biodiversity Institute of Costa Rica is "to promote a greater awareness of the value of biodiversity as a means to ensure its conservation and improve the quality of life of human beings."

The park includes over 600 species of plants, 50 species of birds, and the habitat of sloths, snakes, iguanas, and turtles. There is also a butterfly farm. If you're interested in Entomology, you'll be glad to learn that the park includes a museum with over 3 million insects.

Experiences

You can head to the Museum of Cultures (Museo de Cultura) for a little more cultural immersion. The museum is placed in a remodeled old traditional home that was built sometime between 1885 and 1887. The place has been furnished to include the day-to-day tools to represent the construction and architecture of a coffee estate.

The house was built by using adobe. This construction method relies on using interlaced twigs and reeds and then adding wet soil and wicker to stick the build together. The house is a time machine that takes you through life in rural Costa Rica and shows how the traditional natives lived their daily lives.

While there, you don't just get to walk around and admire the displays and pictures; there are workshops you can participate in. For instance, there is a restaurant that serves traditional Costa Rican meals, where you can take part in a cooking workshop, learn how to make their traditional food, and taste your handiwork.

Shopping Guide in Santo Domingo

Santo Domingo is not without its urban attractions. You can spend a day in Paseo de las Flores, a huge commercial construct with must-visit shopping centers in all of the areas of Heredia. The center has everything you would need in a city: traditional restaurants, fast food, and shops. Essentially, it is a nice place to spend a laid-back afternoon shopping for souvenirs.

Transport in Heredia

Several well-received travel companies in Heredia offer transportation services. Among them are the Costa Rica Trip Guide and Transportes Vitratur.

Again, using the sightseeing buses to get around is probably the most budget-friendly and carries with it a lot of perks and offers.

Make sure you plan ahead when choosing the sites you wish to visit. Even though the local buses run daily and nightly, there are rush hours when you may not be able to book a seat. In that case, you can opt to use a taxi, which can be a bit more expensive than the former option.

Where to Eat

Among the favored locations to dine are La Carretica-Santa Lucia, the KATTA pub, and La Candelaria.

Accommodations

The top picks for hotels in Heredia include Cariari Bed and Breakfast, Hotel Chalet Tirol, and the AC Hotel by Marriot Heredia Belen.

Shopping Guide

An option that comes highly recommended is the Paseo De Las Flores shopping mall. You can also head to the Atlantic Tienda and the Centro de Aventura for gifts and souvenirs.

Chapter 8: The Caribbean Coast (Limon Province)

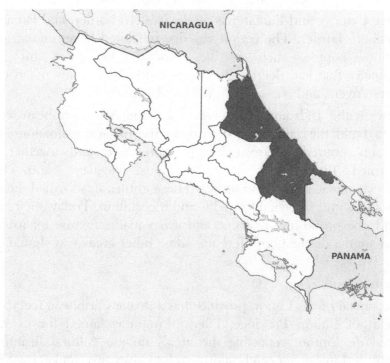

Escape city life to the true Carribean Coast.
TUBS, CC BY-SA 4.0 <https://creativecommons.org/licenses/by-sa/4.0>, via Wikimedia Commons, https://commons.wikimedia.org/wiki/File:Costa_Rica_administrative_divisions_-_de_-_monochrome.svg

If you picked Limón Province of the Caribbean Coast to visit, you made the right choice. Forget your typical Costa Rica postcard with surfers and toucans; Limón is on a whole different level. The Province lounges snuggly on Costa Rica's eastern Caribbean coast, covering an area of 9,189 km2 with a population of up to 400,000. It's considered one of the country's most immaculate and green regions. The province is the perfect place to visit when you want to be away from city life and be surrounded by the awesomeness of nature. The land features everything from mangrove wetlands to towering mountains. Limón harbors many thriving artists and musicians, standing tall as the center of Costa Rica's Afro-Caribbean culture.

Historical and Background Information about Limón Province

Limon is listed among the seven provinces in Costa Rica and shares boundaries with Nicaragua on the northern border, provinces like Heredia, Cartago, and Puntarenas on the western border, and Panama on the southern border. The region was first inhabited by several groups of indigenous people, such as the Cabécar, Terrabas, and Bribri, communities that had deep connections to the land. They relied on the rainforest, rivers, and coastal areas for livelihoods.

Between the 19th and 20th centuries, some Afro-Caribbean workers came to build the railroad and work in the banana plantations. More immigrants poured in from Europe and Asia, and together, they transformed Limón with their traditions, language, and culture, introducing music genres and dishes. These immigrants formed their own organizations and struggled for rights and recognition. Today, the region is known to be proud and resilient, and it has made a name for itself as a popular tourist destination. Here are some other areas you should check out:

Puerto Limón

The capital of the Limon province has a strong Caribbean feel to it. As the heart of Limón Province, Puerto Limón is famed for its vibrant Carnaval de Limón, reflecting the area's unique cultural fusion. The Carnaval de Limón is a celebration that lasts over two weekends. Visitors love the city's historical architecture, bustling markets, and the nearby Playa Bonita.

Did You Know?

- Puerto Limón was founded in 1870 as a port for exporting bananas.
- The Carnaval de Limón celebration is kicked off every October 12th with a children's parade on the opening day and a major parade on October 20th.
- A carnival Queen is elected and crowned at the carnival.

Main Attractions in Puerto Limón

Parque Vargas: This is an excellent place to sit and relax, enjoying the laid-back vibe of the town. It is also where most of the action takes place. The park comes with some great views, a lovely gazebo, and a commemorative statue.

Transport: The transportation options are buses, shuttle flights, and taxis. You shouldn't have much trouble moving around these parts.

Experiences: You can take part in the Ports of Call Tours, as well as cultural and theme Tours, luxury and special occasions, and nightlife.

Places to Eat in Puerto Limón

1. **Restaurante Kalisi** – This is one of the restaurants in the area dedicated to tourists, so you are sure to experience the Caribbean coast and its dishes.

   Address: Calle 6 between Avenues 3 & 4, Puerto Limón, Costa Rica

2. **Soda El Patty** – This is a five-star rated restaurant in the area with the best kind of Caribbean dishes you'll love.

   Address: XXV9+F3C, Limón Province, Limon, Costa Rica

Places to Shop in Puerto Limón

1. **Wolf Mall** – This shopping mall has everything you'll need to make your stay comfortable.

   Address: Limón Province, Limon, Costa Rica

2. **Rising Sun Plaza**

   Address: XXV9+375, Limón Province, Limon, Costa Rica

Entertainment

Puerto Limon has a very different nightlife to the other areas of the Limon Province. Their bars and clubs are more laid back, geared toward reggae lovers. Their music style will have you bobbing your head and tapping your feet to the beat when you get an opportunity to visit. Some of the spots you should visit are:

1. **Bar Casa Rosa** – an excellent place to stop if you love dancing and good music.
2. **Bar El Ganzo** – You should stop here if you're a fan of sitting outdoors, enjoying the cool breeze, and watching live bands sing the night away.

Leisure and Sports: There's a variety of leisure activities you can engage in in this city. There are water sports, sport fishing, bird watching, and snorkeling.

Accommodations

1. **Westfalia Beach Hotel** – This three-star hotel features well-furnished rooms, cable TVs, free Wi-Fi, complimentary breakfast, beach access, and an outdoor pool.

    Address: 2 km to the south of the Limón airport, Limón, Costa Rica

2. **Hotel Playa Bonita** – This is a two-star casual lodging with low-key dining, complimentary breakfast, a clean pool, free Wi-Fi, and free parking space.

    Address: 500 meters south of Playa Bonita, Limón, Barrio Cangrejos, 1000, Costa Rica

Tortuguero

Accessible only by boat or small aircraft, Tortuguero is a paradise for wildlife enthusiasts. It's known for the Tortuguero National Park, a crucial nesting site for endangered sea turtles and a sanctuary teeming with diverse flora and fauna. The little village is a must-see during your journey in Costa Rica. It will surely turn your trip into an unforgettable experience.

Did You Know?

- The region began to develop with the arrival of the railroad to Costa Rica in 1890.

- The Caribbean Conservation Corporation (CCC) was created in Tortuguero by Dr. Archie Carr in the 1950s.

Main Attractions in Tortuguero

Tortuguero National Park: The magnificent park is on the country's Caribbean coast, Limon Province. If you want to find your way there, use private or public transport to get to La Pavona jetty, where you will find boats going to the park. At the park, there are lots of activities you can enjoy. The park is home to various wildlife, including monkeys, jaguars, sea turtles, and sloths. It is a must-stop place in Costa Rica. You can also go on the 3-hour canoe tours through the National Park for sightseeing.

Tortuguero National Park.
caspar s, CC BY 2.0 <https://creativecommons.org/licenses/by/2.0>, via Wikimedia Commons: https://commons.wikimedia.org/wiki/File:Tortuguero_National_Park_(5596782460).jpg

Opening Hours:
- Every day from 6 AM to 12 PM and from 1 PM to 4 PM.

As of the writing of this book, the aforementioned are the regular opening hours. However, please always double-check the opening hours online should there have been any slight change in their schedule.

Transport: Tortuguero is located in a remote area of the Caribbean coast, which is mostly accessed by boats or by air. A car service can drive you around when you're in the town, but if you wish to visit the Tortuguero National Park, you will have to go by boat.

Experiences: Van and boat tours, car rental, and the all-inclusive package: 2 nights and 3 days in Tortuguero from San Jose.

Places to Eat in Tortuguero

1. **Restaurante Mi Niño**
   Address: 70205 Limon Pococi, Costa Rica
2. **Miss Miriam's Restaurant** – Here, you can get very tasty and well-prepared meals. The restaurant is ranked in the top 10 restaurants in Tortuguero.
   Address: GFRX+J2G, Costado Norte de Plaza Futbol, Limón Province, Roxana, Costa Rica
3. **Soda Doña Mary** - This is a vegan-friendly restaurant.
   Address: 6839+MMX, Limón Province, Guacimo, Costa Rica

Places to Shop in Tortuguero

1. **Souvenir Pura Vida** – The best place to go when shopping for cool souvenirs.
   Address: Main Street, Limón Province, Costa Rica
2. **Super Turtles** – This is a supermarket.
   Address: GFVW+4HW, Limón Province, Roxana, Costa Rica

Entertainment

Tortuguero Beach – You can stroll along the shore and watch turtles while listening to soft music echoing around the beach.

Accommodations

1. **Tortuguero Natural B&B** – They've got colorful rooms, balconies, a casual restaurant, free Wi-Fi, and free parking spaces.
   Address: 200 meters east of Cabinas Miss Miriam, next to the Adventist Church, Limón, Costa Rica
2. **Mawamba Lodge Tortuguero** – The hotel is set along a beach on the Caribbean Sea and offers free Wi-Fi, free breakfast, free parking, beach access, and laundry service.
   Address: Tortuguero Canals, Limón, Pococí, Costa Rica

Cahuita

Cahuita is a region in the Limón Province famous for the Cahuita National Park, with its picturesque beaches, coral reefs for snorkeling, and a laid-back atmosphere influenced by its Afro-Caribbean community.

Did You Know?
- There are colorful souvenir shops, reggae bars, and local eateries lining the Av. Negra, the village's main street.
- The Cahuita National Park is like a giant aquarium but way cooler. The coral reefs are bursting with life, and you may even spot a nurse shark.

Main Attractions in Cahuita

Cahuita National Park – The national park is one of the most stunning destinations in the whole of Costa Rica. It's tourist-friendly and open to all.

Cahuita National Park.
Pavel Kirillov from St.Petersburg, Russia, CC BY-SA 2.0 <https://creativecommons.org/licenses/by-sa/2.0>, via Wikimedia Commons:
https://commons.wikimedia.org/wiki/File:View_of_Cahuita_National_Park,_CR_(9901357883).jpg

- **Opens:** Every day from 8:00 am to 4:00 pm.

Transport: In Cahuita, there are taxis and shuttles, but if you plan on exploring the town for its local sights, then walking, biking, and taking buses are the best ways to go. Plus, they're less expensive.

Experiences: Water tours, multi-day tours, walking tours, cultural and theme tours, and glorious nightlife.

Places to Eat in Cahuita

1. **Restaurante Bar La Peruanita**

   Address: Cahuita Main Road, Limón, Cahuita, Costa Rica

2. **Rincón del Amor**

   Address: 40 meters north of the police station. Next to the community hall, Calle Central, Limón, Cahuita, 70403, Costa Rica

3. **Kawe Restaurant**

   Address: P5P5+RX9, Limón Province, Cahuita, Costa Rica

Places to Shop in Cahuita

1. **Super Negro Cahuita (Grocery Store)**

   Address: P5P5+C7C, Limón Province, Cahuita, Costa Rica

2. **Super Vaz #2** -This is the largest of the supermarkets in Cahuita. You can get anything you need here when you visit Cahuita.

   Address: P5P6+Q32, Main Road, Limón Province, Cahuita, Costa Rica

Entertainment

1. **Chao's Bar** – If you find yourself within this axis of the Caribbean coast and need a pleasant open-air space for beer, seafood, and fries, you should certainly come here.

   Address: Playa Negra, Limón, Cahuita, 7302, Costa Rica

2. **Coco's Bar** – Try Coco's Bar for lively reggae, soccer, and samba blast weekends. You might find an assemblage of dogs on the veranda, but don't be scared; they are harmless and are allowed there to show the rhythm of life.

   Address: P5Q5+4J9, Limón Province, Cahuita, Costa Rica

Leisure and Sports: You can go shipwreck diving, snorkeling, or chill out on the black sand beaches.

Accommodations

1. **Playa Negra Guesthouse** – Tropical guesthouse near the beach with comfortable accommodations, private terraces, and well-maintained grounds.

    Address: Playa Negra de, 100 Meters north of the soccer field, imón, Cahuita, 70403, Costa Rica

2. **Cahuita Inn** – A great location with an excellent Italian restaurant on-site. Their rooms are very clean, and they have a nice beach view.

    Address: 50 meters east of the police station, Limón, Cahuita, Costa Rica

3. **Le Colibri Rouge Hotel Cabins** – This small-budget hotel has clean rooms and very comfortable beds.

    Address: 300 meters from the park entrance, C. Puerto Vargas, Limón, Cahuita, 7302, Costa Rica

Puerto Viejo de Talamanca

Known for its vibrant nightlife, excellent surf spots, and beautiful beaches like Playa Negra, the cultural diversity here in Puerto Viejo de Talamanca contributes to an array of culinary delights, making it popular among younger travelers.

Did You Know?

- Puerto Viejo was once a sleepy fishing village but has now been transformed into a popular tourist destination.
- The Playa Negra stretches over 10 kilometers between Puerto Viejo town and Cahuita National Park.

Main Attractions

1. **Playa Puerto Viejo** – This is one of the beaches on this axis and one of the top tourist attractions of the city.

Playa Puerto Viejo.

Esteban Folch, CC BY-SA 4.0 <https://creativecommons.org/licenses/by-sa/4.0>, via Wikimedia Commons: https://commons.wikimedia.org/wiki/File:Playa_de_Puerto_Viejo,_Lim%C3%B3n,_Costa_Rica.jpg

   Opens: 24 hours

2. **Old Harbor Art and Craft Market** – If you have a thing for handmade products and crafts, then you should definitely go to the Old Harbor. All the products displayed are exclusive and handmade by local artists and artisans.

   Opens: Friday, Saturday, and Sunday, from 3:00 pm to 8:00 pm.

3. **Talamanca Viewpoint** – This is one of the famous tourist attractions in Puerto Viejo. This place has a very impressive view; you definitely want to see it.

   Opens: 24 hours

Transport: Biking is one of the most popular ways to move around Puerto Viejo de Talamanca. If that's not your thing, there are also buses, taxis – and sometimes tuks –available.

Experiences: Hiking tours, food, wine and nightlife, waterfall experience, and chocolate tour.

Places to Eat

1. **Grow Puerto Viejo** – A restaurant designed to give you a unique experience of delicious and healthy flavors.

    Address: Beach Front, Puerto Viejo Center, Limón, Talamanca, Costa Rica

2. **Lidia's Place Restaurant** – this five-star restaurant has you fully covered food-wise!

    Address: M64X+C44, Limón Province, Puerto Viejo de Talamanca, Costa Rica

3. **Black and White** – From seafood to pasta, a steak house, and a good Caribbean dish, this restaurant offers a world of deliciousness.

    Address: C. de Veronicas Place, Puerto Viejo de Talamanca, Limon, Costa Rica

Places to Shop

1. **Tienda del Mar** – This two-in-one store is sprawled around a street corner in the center of town. It specializes in colorful batik clothing of all sizes, sandals, wood carvings, and ceramics.

    Address: Av. 71, Limón, Puerto Viejo de Talamanca, Costa Rica

2. **Feria Agrícola y Artesanel** – This is the town's Saturday morning market, where you can stock up on fresh fruits and veggies for your weekend beach picnics. The shopping center is in the building just south of the bus stop.

Entertainment

1. **Puerto Pirata Tiki Bar** – The location sits right on the beach, with amazing panoramic views of the Caribbean Ocean. The bar has a vegan-friendly restaurant, offering good music and live band entertainment on certain nights.

    Address: C. 215, Limón, Puerto Viejo de Talamanca, Costa Rica

2. **Johnny's Place** – This cozy spot has excellent cocktails, live music, and outdoor seating with a perfect view of the ocean.

Address: M65V+5X6, Av. 73, Limón, Puerto Viejo de Talamanca, Costa Rica

Leisure and Sports: In Puerto Viejo de Talamanca, you get the opportunity to show off your biking skills, go scuba diving or surfing, or join hiking tours.

Accommodations

1. **Hotel Puerto Viejo** – A three-star hotel that offers free Wi-Fi, paid breakfast, free parking, and an on-site restaurant.

   Address: M65X+64Q, Calle 73, 256, Limón, Puerto Viejo de Talamanca, 70403, Costa Rica

2. **Hotel Casa Vito** – A nice hotel with spacious rooms, a fantastic beach view, and delicious breakfast. Don't miss out.

   Address: M743+XRR, Limón Province, Puerto Viejo de Talamanca, Costa Rica

Manzanillo

This serene fishing village is perfect for those seeking peace and pristine nature. It's the gateway to the Gandoca Manzanillo Wildlife Refuge, offering superb hiking, snorkeling, and the chance to experience Costa Rica's indigenous cultures.

Did You Know?

- The Manzanillo beach isn't just a beach. It's a tapestry woven with rainforest, mangroves, and coral reefs.
- Manzanillo prioritizes sustainability, offering eco-lodges and guesthouses built with local resources and powered by renewable energy.

Main Attractions

1. **National Parks and Private Refugees**
   - Gandoca-Manzanillo Wildlife Refuge
     - **Open:** Every day from 6:30 am to 3:00 pm.
2. **Beaches:**
   - Manzanillo
     - **Open:** 24/7

- Playa Chiquita
  - **Open:** 24/7
- Punta Uva
  - **Open:** 24/7
3. **Museums and Gardens**
   - Cacao Trails
     - **Open:** Every day from 8 am to 4 pm.
   - Finca La Isla Botanical Garden
     - **Open:** Friday to Monday from 10 am to 4 pm, closed Tuesday, Wednesday, and Thursday.

Transport: The bus service in Manzanillo is less frequent. Since the area between Puerto Viejo and Manzanillo is compact and mostly flat, a bicycle rental is an exceptional means of travel.

Experiences: Sightseeing tours, surfing, wildlife watching, turtle tours, and chocolate tours.

Places to Eat in Manzanillo

1. **Colores Restaurant and Beach Lounge –** This should be your next stop for international dishes, seafood, and traditional Costa Rican dishes.
   Address: Manzanillo center, Limón, Manzanillo, 70403, Costa Rica
2. **Restaurant 4th Generation -** For delicious meals and great cocktails.
   Address: J8JR+XPX, Limón Province, Manzanillo, Costa Rica

Places to Shop in Manzanillo

1. **Supermercado Manzanillo** – Grocery Store.
2. **Mini Super Más Por Menos**
3. **Minimarket**

Entertainment

1. **Natural Bar**
   Address: Enter via Las Veraneras, next to Super, Limón Province, Manzanillo, Costa Rica

2. Licorera Manzanillo

   Address: J8JR+XW5 frente a, cabinas Maxe's, Limón, Manzanillo, Costa Rica

Leisure and Sports: You can enjoy activities like snorkeling, kayaking, scuba diving, chocolate tours, and surfing in Manzanillo.

Accommodations

1. **Almonds and Corals Jungle Resort.** A family-run lodge in the Gandoca Manzanillo Wildlife Refuge that offers free Wi-Fi, complimentary breakfast, beach access, and laundry service.

   Address: 2KM Antes de Manzanillo, Limón, Manzanillo, Costa Rica

2. **Manzanillo Caribbean Resort.** This luxurious resort offers free Wi-Fi, free parking, breakfast, an outdoor pool, and comfortable rooms with good air conditioning.

   Address: Enter via Recope Recreation Center, Limón Province, Manzanillo, 70403, Costa Rica

3. **Cabinas Manzanillo Caribe.** Good restaurant, kitchens in some rooms, free Wi-Fi, pet-friendly, and free parking.

   Address: 150 meters south of Minaet en Manzanillo, Limón, Manzanillo, 70403, Costa Rica

Sixaola

While primarily a transit town at the Panama border, Sixaola offers its unique charm, with opportunities to explore nearby banana plantations and enjoy the scenic beauty of the surrounding regions. Include a few images of these plantations, too, if possible. They will provide an interesting view into the culture of Costa Rica as a whole.

Did You Know?

- There are only about 1823 citizens settled in this region.
- In Sixaola, you can learn about sustainable farming practices and discover the secrets of bean-to-bar chocolate at a local cocoa farm.

Main Attractions

The Sixaola Bridge. This bridge plays a significant role as a landmark and gives you a glimpse into the history of the culture and area as you walk across it.

Sixaola Bridge.
*Arturo Sotillo from La Canada, CA, USA, CC BY-SA 2.0
<https://creativecommons.org/licenses/by-sa/2.0>, via Wikimedia Commons:
https://commons.wikimedia.org/wiki/File:Sixaola_Bridge.jpg*

- **Open:** 6:00 am to 11:45 pm.

Transport: You can find a bus any time at Sixaola. Some shuttles and taxis carry you from one point to the other.

Experiences: Boogie boarding, surfing, or diving, joining the canopy tour, and visiting an Indian reserve.

Places to Eat in Sixaola

1. **Soda la Terraza**
   Address: G92P+R7X Terminal de Buses, Limón, Sixaola, Costa Rica
2. **Fusion Restaurante**
   Address: G93P+C39, Limón Province, Sixaola, Costa Rica

Places to Shop in Sixaola

1. **El Puente Grocery**
   Address: G92P+X7G, Limón Province, Sixaola, Costa Rica
2. **Supermercado Sixaola**
   Address: Sixaola Center, Limón, Sixaola, Costa Rica

Leisure and Sports: The town of Sixaola is quite small and doesn't have many leisure and sports activities compared to the other neighboring towns.

Accommodations

1. **Soda y Cabinas Kániki:** This local inn offers free WiFi service, free parking, paid breakfast, and room service.
   Address: 70101 Gandoca, from the school, 550 meters following the road to Limon Beach, Talamanca - Sixaola, 70101, Costa Rica
2. **Cabinas El Mango:** This is another place in the region where you can lodge during your time in Sixaola.
   Address: Limón Province, Bribri, Costa Rica

Limón Province's Caribbean Coast in Costa Rica is a captivating region with a rich history and plenty of incredible attractions. It is the perfect blend of natural beauty and cultural wealth. This region has networks of beaches, rivers, ecotourists, and wildlife conservation, which have become popular tourist destinations. The people there are primarily youthful and free-spirited, and they treat tourists kindly. From Puerto Limón, the Province's capital, to Sixaola, which is primarily a transit town to Panama, you will indeed have the experience of a lifetime cruising through Limon Province.

Chapter 9: Itineraries and Programs

Now that you know all the great places to visit in Costa Rica and the fun activities to keep you entertained, you are probably wondering how to make the best of your vacation. This chapter includes different itineraries and programs so you can have a great time in Costa Rica.

Disclaimer: All itineraries are suggestions. Please feel free to mix and match as you see fit and to change chronological day orders based on your current location.

Having an itinerary can help you make the best of your vacation.
https://unsplash.com/photos/text-R4sP8_Bq0Bw?utm_content=creditShareLink&utm_medium=referral&utm_source=unsplash

Brief San Jose Tour 1 (1 day)

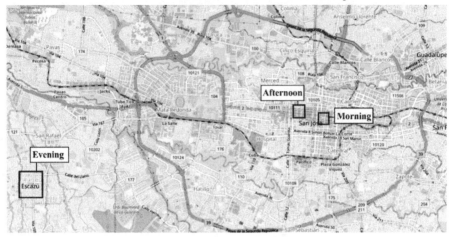

Brief San Jose Tour (1 day).
OpenStreetMap Contributors https://www.openstreetmap.org

Morning: Take a guided tour of the Costa Rican National Theater, then people-watch on the Plaza de la Cultura until lunch.

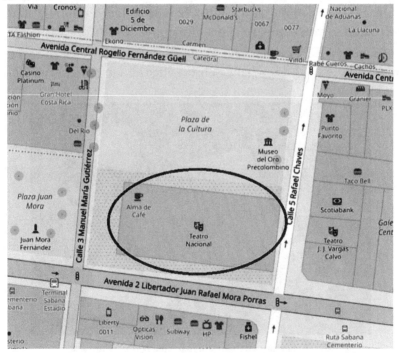

Costa Rican National Theater.
OpenStreetMap Contributors https://www.openstreetmap.org

Afternoon: Fill up your energy tanks at the San Jose Central Market and spend two hours (or more) exploring downtown and shopping for souvenirs. When you get tired, grab a cup of coffee and snacks at Spoon.

Spoon addresses:
- Av. Central, San José, El Carmen, 10101, Costa Rica
- WWMF+GFC, Rogelio Fernández Güell, San José, El Carmen, 10101, Costa Rica

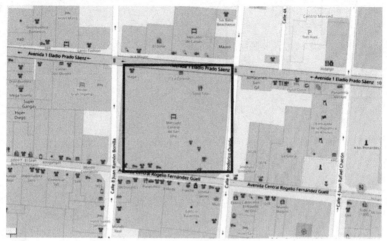

San Jose Central Market.
OpenStreetMap Contributors https://www.openstreetmap.org

Evening: After freshening up at your lodgings, drive to Escazu (8.5km away) and have an authentic Costa Rican dining experience at Posada de las Brujas.

Posada de las Brujas Address: WV97+V93, San José Province, Escazu, Costa Rica

Escazu.
OpenStreetMap Contributors https://www.openstreetmap.org

Brief San Jose Tour 2 (1 day)

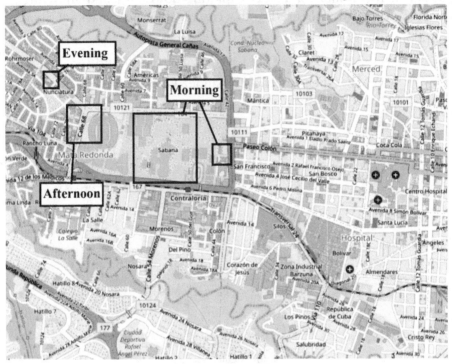

Brief San Jose Tour 2 (1 day).
OpenStreetMap Contributors https://www.openstreetmap.org

Morning: If breakfast isn't included at your lodgings, have a hearty breakfast at Soda Tapia. Then, head to Parque Metropolitano La Sabana to explore the lake and the surrounding trails, along with the Museum of Costa Rican Art to view the exhibits and the remnants of an old airport.

Soda Tapia address: C. 42, San José, San Francisco, Costa Rica

Afternoon: After a filling lunch at Cervecera Republica, where you can feast your eyes on the stadium and emerge into the local culture, go back to your lodgings to freshen up.

Cervecera Republica address: West side of San Jose National Stadium, 104, San José Province, San José, Nunciatura, Costa Rica

Evening: Rest a little, then head up to Furca to enjoy a delicious meal with a variety of drinks.

Furca address: Across from Lafise bank, WVRQ+4C9, Nunciatura, San José, Costa Rica Sabana Norte. 200 metros west of Scotiabank, San José, Nunciatura, 10108, Costa Rica

5-Day Itinerary for San Jose

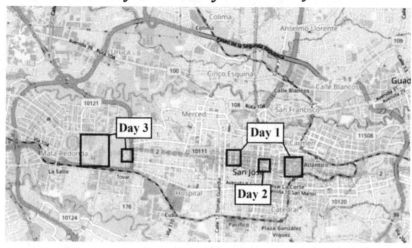

Days 1 to 3.
OpenStreetMap Contributors https://www.openstreetmap.org

Day 1:

Morning: Arrival in San Jose, check into accommodation. Breakfast at a local restaurant. Visit the Jade Museum and the Plaza de la Democracia.

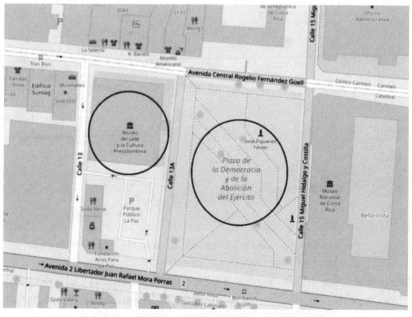

Jade Museum (left) and Plaza de la Democracia (right)
OpenStreetMap Contributors https://www.openstreetmap.org

Afternoon: Check out the San Jose Central Market (see the map in image 0) and take a guided city tour to learn more about its culture and history.

Evening: Explore San Jose's electric nightlife by visiting the Astro Bar.

Address: WWMP+MRX, Av 5, San José, Empalme, 10101, Costa Rica

Day 2:

Morning: Breakfast at a local restaurant.

Afternoon: Visit the Costa Rican National Theater (see the map in image 0), which has been the host of several performances since its establishment.

Evening: Enjoy a relaxing dinner at Sabor Italiano, a short walk away from Teatro Nacional.

Sabor Italiano Address: WWMG+P7R, Av. 1, San José, El Carmen, 10101, Costa Rica

Day 3:

Morning: Breakfast at a local deli, followed by a visit to the Museum of Costa Rican Art.

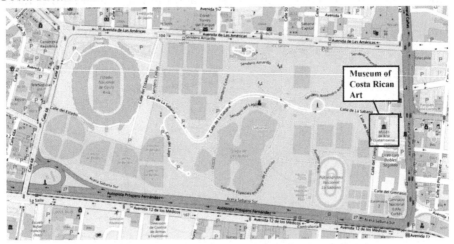

Parque Metropolitano La Sabana with Museum of Costa Rican Art.
OpenStreetMap Contributors https://www.openstreetmap.org

Afternoon: Spend the day at Parque Metropolitano La Sabana. It has leafy areas, perfect spots for picnics, and a museum featuring regional art.

Evening: End the night at a Costa Rican dinner show at Ram Luna or Mirador Tiquicia.

Ram Luna address (14km away): Mirador, De la Iglesia de Aserrí, 5km north, road to Tarbaca about Ruta 209, San José Province, Aserri, Costa Rica

Mirador Tiquicia address (12.5km away): Bebedero, San Antonio, Costa Rica

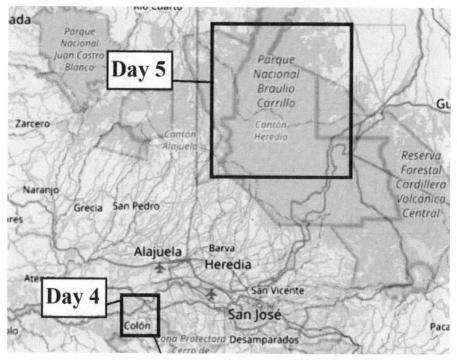

Days 4 to 5.
OpenStreetMap Contributors https://www.openstreetmap.org

Day 4:

Morning: Breakfast at a local restaurant.

Afternoon: Visit Costa Rica's Craft Brewing Company.

Address: WQJ9+X59, San José, Brasil, Brasil de Mora, Costa Rica

Evening: End the evening with dinner at a local restaurant.

Day 5:

Morning: Travel to Braulio Carrillo National Park (50km away) for a rainforest aerial tram tour. This tour takes 7 hours, and most departure times start at 6am.

Evening: Return to San Jose and end your stay with a celebration at one of the city's local bars.

Guanacaste Province Tour (5 days)

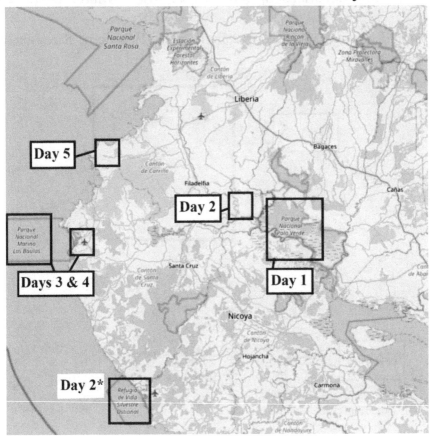

Guanacaste Province Tour.
OpenStreetMap Contributors https://www.openstreetmap.org

Day 1: Settling and Exploring the Area

Morning: Arrive at the hotel near Palo Verde National Park and settle in, preparing for your upcoming adventures.

Afternoon: Explore the park and take a boat tour to really enjoy the experience. Later, find a restaurant to sample the local cuisine.

Evening: Go souvenir shopping and explore the local art and architecture.

Day 2: Wetlands and Rainforest Exploration

Morning and afternoon: Take a boat ride or cultural tour of the Hacienda El Viejo Wetlands. Here, you can also have an authentic rum tour and experience the essence of Guanacaste tradition.

* If you are visiting during one of the many rainy months, you can close off your day and tour with a visit to Ostional Wildlife Refuge to witness nesting Olive Ridley Sea Turtles and see baby turtles emerge.

Evening: Enjoy a lavish meal at a local restaurant and relax.

Day 3: Wildlife Tour

Morning: Head to Tamarindo, check into your accommodation, and explore the Marino Las Baulas National Park.

Afternoon: Explore Tamarindo and enjoy a nice lunch with a spectacular view.

Evening: After a short boat ride through the estuary, head back to your accommodations for dinner and relaxation.

Day 4: A Day of Adventures

Morning: Have a filling breakfast, then take the Guachipelin combo adventure tour (a tour that lasts almost 10 hours) from Tamarindo, starting with horseback riding.

Afternoon: After lunch (included in this specific tour), continue your adventures with white water tubing.

Evening: End your day with a mud bath before returning to your lodgings.

Day 5: Waterfront Exploration

Morning: Go ziplining at the Diamante Adventure Park for an adventure-filled start to the day.

Afternoon: Take a surfing lesson at Tamarindo.

Evening: Head to one of the nearby beaches or chill at the hotel pool, depending on what amenities you have available at your accommodations.

Puntarenas Province Tour (7-8 days)

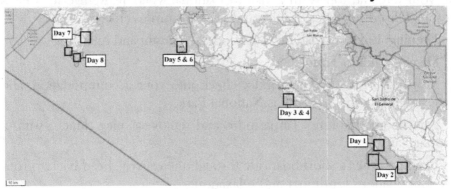

Puntarenas Province Tour.
OpenStreetMap Contributors https://www.openstreetmap.org

Note: To really get a head start on this itinerary, it would be best to arrive in Costa Rica early in the morning. There are many ways to get to Uvita from Juan Santamaría International Airport, but we'd advise taking a shuttle since it would be the fastest way so you can start your day early on. The shuttle takes almost 3 hours.

Day 1: Exploring Uvita

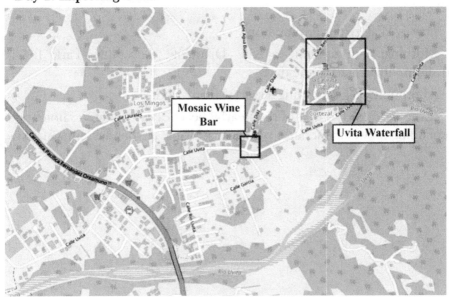

Mosaic Wine Bar and Uvita Waterfall.
OpenStreetMap Contributors https://www.openstreetmap.org

Morning: Explore the city and settle in.

Afternoon: After having lunch at Mosaic Wine Bar, head to the Uvita Waterfall and enjoy the day.

Mosaic Wine Bar address: 600 meters past the BCR towards the Uvita Waterfall, Provincia de Puntarenas, Uvita, 60504, Costa Rica

Evening: Take a nap or watch the sunset on the city shores.

Day 2: Touring Uvita

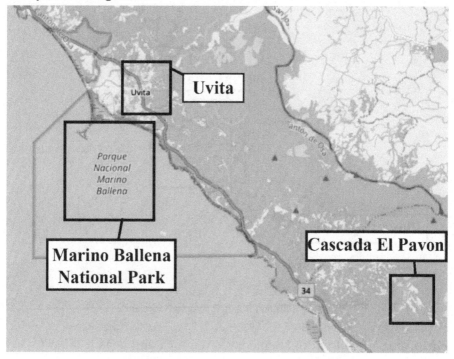

Marino Ballena National Park and Cascada el Pavon.
OpenStreetMap Contributors https://www.openstreetmap.org

Morning and Afternoon: Set out on a whale-watching or Cano Island snorkeling tour (about 90 minutes on a boat leaving from Uvita), depending on the season (the former is available from January through March and from July through September).

Alternative: Explore Marino Ballena National Park and enjoy the beaches. You can swim, stand-up paddle and more.

Late afternoon/Evening: If time allows, drive to the charming Cascada El Pavon waterfall (20 minutes away from Uvita).

Day 3: Heading to Manuel Antonio (1 hour from Uvita)

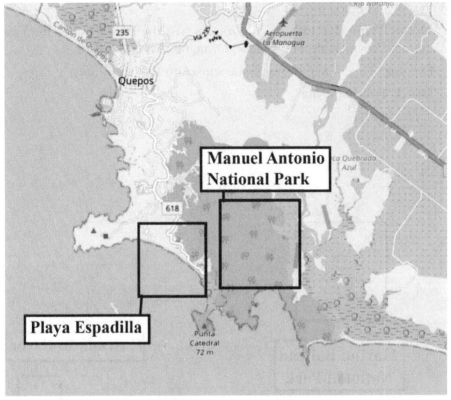

Playa Espadilla and Manuel Antonio National Park.
OpenStreetMap Contributors https://www.openstreetmap.org

Morning and afternoon: Settle in, have lunch and head to Playa Espadilla to relax on the beach or go swimming.

Evening: Have dinner at one of the restaurants near the beach to watch the sunset over the water.

Day 4: Wildlife Adventures in Manuel Antonio

Morning: Start your day by touring the Manuel Antonio National Park and see the wildlife inhabiting its swaying palm trees and perfect white sand beaches.

Afternoon: After lunch, you can continue walking or hiking in the park or relax on the beaches, hanging around with monkeys and sloths.

Evening: Relax with dinner and wine at one of the nearby restaurants/hotels that offer a spectacular view of the national park.

Day 5: Exploring Jaco

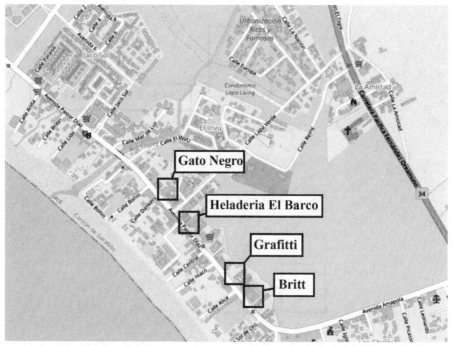

Jaco Restaurant Map.
OpenStreetMap Contributors https://www.openstreetmap.org

Morning: Head for a healthy breakfast/brunch at Britt Café and Bakery.

Address: Jaco Walk Provincia de Puntarenas Garabito, 61101, Costa Rica

Afternoon: Head onto the beach to take surf lessons or just take a leisurely walk enjoying the views.

Evening: Explore the rest of town and have dinner and a few drinks to celebrate the beginning of your holiday at one of the many places with happy hours and special deals for tourists.

Day 6: More Jaco Adventures

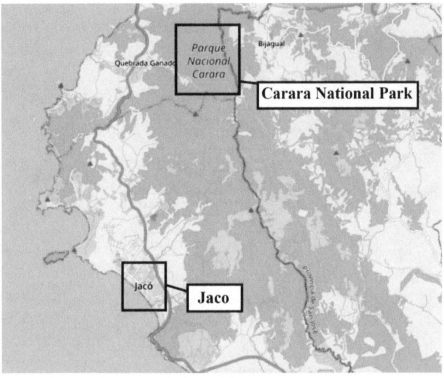

Carara National Park.
OpenStreetMap Contributors https://www.openstreetmap.org

Morning: Explore Carara National Park or go horseback riding.

Afternoon: Have lunch at El Gato Negro on Pastor Diaz Avenue, followed by gelato at the Heladeria El Barco.

El Gato Negro address: 61101, Provincia de Puntarenas, Jacó, 61101, Costa Rica

Heladeria El Barco address: J97F+H29, Pastor Diaz Ave, Puntarenas Province, Jaco, Costa Rica

Evening: End your day by having dinner at Graffiti.

Address: Jaco Walk Open Air Shopping Center, Avenida Pastor Diaz, Provincia de Puntarenas, Jacó, 61101, Costa Rica

Day 7: Heading to Mal País (5 hours from Jaco, so head out early)

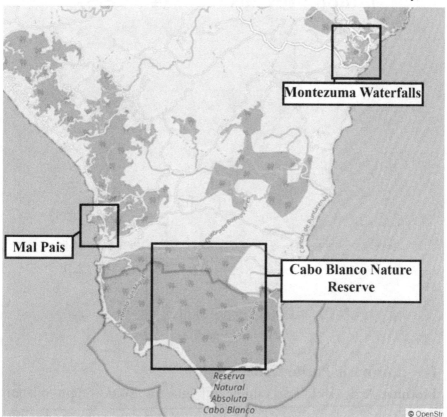

Mal Pais, Cabo Blanco Nature Reserve and Montezuma Waterfalls.
OpenStreetMap Contributors https://www.openstreetmap.org

Morning: Arrive at Mal Pais and settle in, exploring the city.

Early Afternoon and evening: Have a scenic trip to Montezuma Waterfalls, enjoy the relaxed atmosphere, and then return to Mal Pais for dinner and settling down.

Day 8: Wildlife Adventures

Morning and Afternoon: Explore Cabo Blanco Nature Reserve through the famous Sueco Trail (5km to the beach and 5km back, a total of 10km on foot).

Evening: Enjoy the best organic Central American cuisine at one of Mal Pais's laid-back restaurants.

Limon Province Tour (4-5 days)

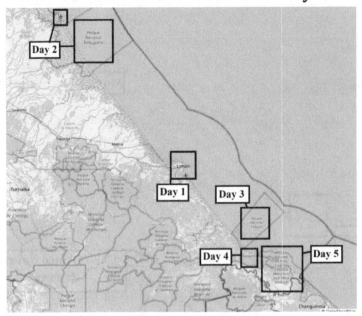

Limon Province Tour.
OpenStreetMap Contributors https://www.openstreetmap.org

Day 1: Arrival in Puerto Limón

Morning: Arrive in Puerto Limón and settle into your accommodation.

Afternoon: Explore the city, visit local markets, and enjoy a beachside lunch featuring Afro-Caribbean cuisine.

Evening: Relax on Playa Bonita, followed by dinner in the city.

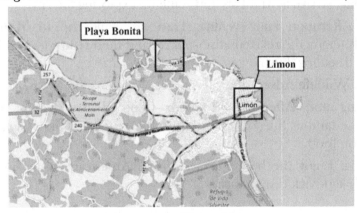

Playa Bonita and Puerto Limón.
OpenStreetMap Contributors https://www.openstreetmap.org

Day 2: Tortuguero Adventure

Early Morning: Depart for Tortuguero, based on your arrangement, via boat or small plane.

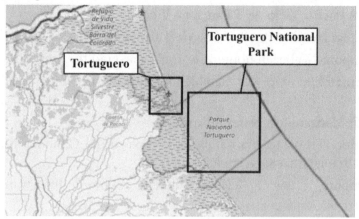

Tortuguero and Tortuguero National Park.
OpenStreetMap Contributors https://www.openstreetmap.org

Late Morning/Afternoon: Take a guided tour of Tortuguero National Park and experience the wildlife. Learn about turtle conservation efforts.

Evening: Return to the lodging area and relax or do a night exploration of turtle nesting (seasonal).

Day 3: Cahuita National Park Excursion

Morning: Travel to Cahuita and embark on a guided hike or snorkeling tour in Cahuita National Park.

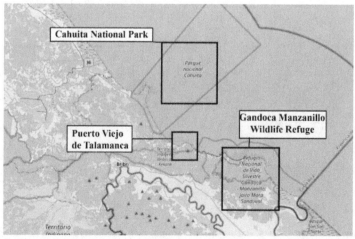

Cahuita National Park, Puerto Viejo de Talamanca and Gandoca Manzanillo Wildlife Refuge.
OpenStreetMap Contributors https://www.openstreetmap.org

Afternoon: Relax on the white-sand beaches and explore the small town of Cahuita.

Evening: Enjoy local Afro-Caribbean dishes at a local restaurant.

Day 4: Puerto Viejo de Talamanca Vibes

Morning: Head to Puerto Viejo de Talamanca.

Afternoon: Go beach hopping or cycling around the area.

Evening: Experience the nightlife and dine in one of the town's vibrant eateries.

Day 5: Manzanillo's Natural Beauty

Morning: Travel to Manzanillo and explore the Gandoca Manzanillo Wildlife Refuge through a guided tour.

Afternoon: Enjoy a leisurely lunch, followed by swimming or snorkeling.

Evening: Return journey to Puerto Limón or next destination.

La Fortuna — Monteverde — Santa Teresa — Gulf of Papagayo Tour (14 days)

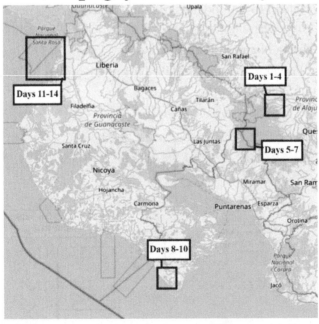

Take a trip across Costa Rica, starting in La Fortuna, then Monteverde, then Santa Teresa and ending with the Gulf of Papagayo.

OpenStreetMap Contributors: https://www.openstreetmap.org

Day 1: Arrival at La Fortuna

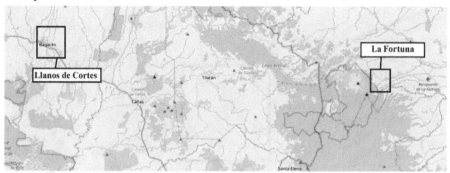

Llanos de Cortes waterfall.
OpenStreetMap Contributors https://www.openstreetmap.org

Morning and Afternoon: Settling in La Fortuna. Check out Llanos de Cortes waterfall between La Fortuna and Liberia (2 hours away).

Evening: Relax at the hotel/accommodation or a nearby restaurant, sampling the local cuisine.

Day 2: Hiking and Visiting Hot Springs

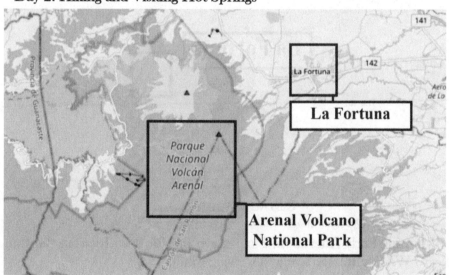

Arenal Volcano National Park.
OpenStreetMap Contributors https://www.openstreetmap.org

Morning: Start your day with the Arenal Volcano National Park.

Afternoon: Take a trip to the hot springs and watch the sunset.

Evening: Head back to your accommodation to relax after a full day of adventures.

Day 3: Floating and Cooking (almost 2 hours away from La Fortuna)

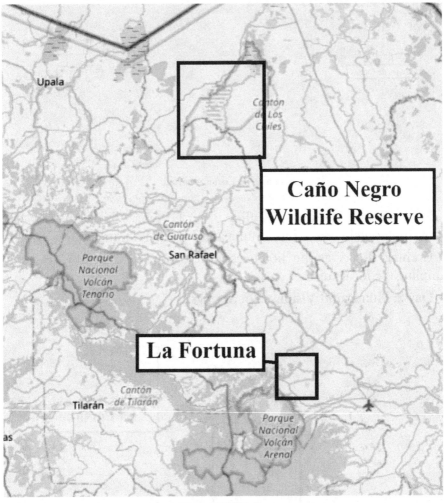

Caño Negro Wildlife Reserve.
OpenStreetMap Contributors https://www.openstreetmap.org

Morning/Early Afternoon: Float down the Rio Frio River in the Caño Negro Wildlife Reserve while observing wildlife.

Late Afternoon/Evening: Take a farm-to-table cooking class to learn the secrets behind the incredible flavors of the local cuisine.

Day 4: Relaxing Day

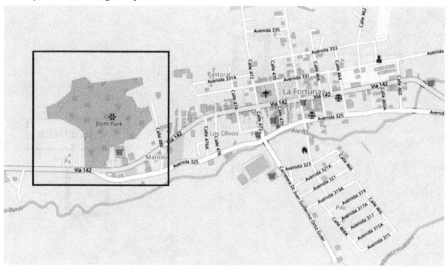

Sloth Park.
OpenStreetMap Contributors https://www.openstreetmap.org

Morning: Have a relaxing morning, chilling by the pool or at a cafe near your accommodation.

Afternoon: Go shopping in La Fortuna and have lunch in town.

Evening: Take a stroll through Sloth Park in the afternoon to see wildlife.

Day 5: Heading to Monteverde (3.5 to 4 hours)

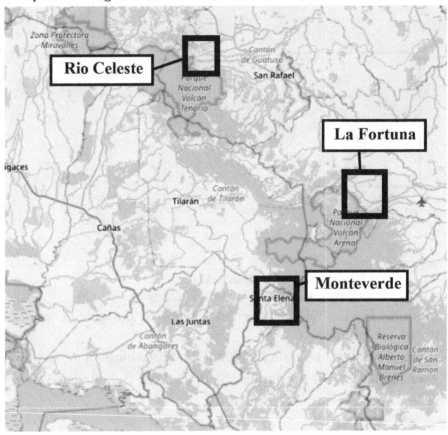

Rio Celeste.
OpenStreetMap Contributors https://www.openstreetmap.org

Note: The drive goes west and then south around Lake Arenal

Morning: As you head to Monteverde, stop by Rio Celeste between La Fortuna and Monteverde to observe the sky-blue river.

Afternoon: Check out the town.

Evening: After dinner at Sabor Tico, go souvenir shopping.

Sabor Tico address: 620, Provincia de Puntarenas, Monteverde, Costa Rica

Day 6: Adventures at Monteverde

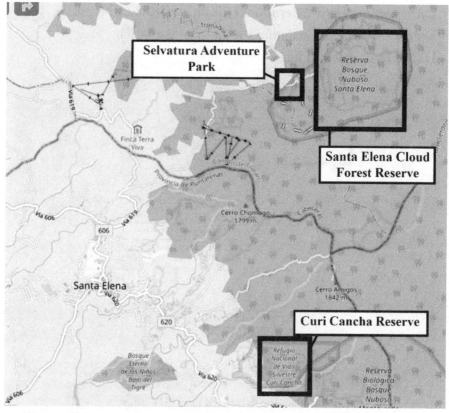

Selvatura Adventure Park, Santa Elena Cloud Forest Reserve and Curi Cancha Reserve.
OpenStreetMap Contributors https://www.openstreetmap.org

Morning: Head to Selvatura Adventure Park for ziplining, hanging bridge adventures, and much more.

Afternoon: After a quick lunch at the park, continue exploring the sloth center, butterfly garden, herpetarium, and insect exhibit.

Evening: Head back to your accommodations to freshen up and have dinner.

Day 7: Strolls and Birdwatching

Morning: Start your day with a morning in Santa Elena Cloud Forest Reserve.

Afternoon: Go birdwatching at Curi Cancha Reserve.

Evening: After dinner, go for a coffee and chocolate tour.

Day 8: Heading to Santa Teresa (4.5 hours by bus, 4 hours driving)
Late Morning/Early Afternoon: Go surfing in Santa Teresa.
Evening: Watch the beautiful sunset from the beach.
Day 9: Horseback Riding

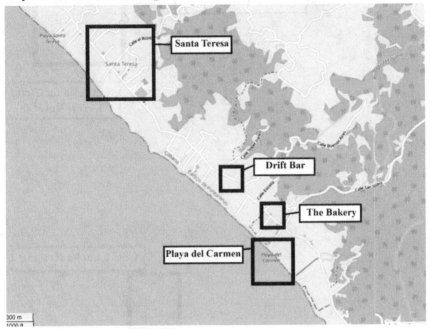

Drift Bar, The Bakery and Playa del Carmen.
OpenStreetMap Contributors https://www.openstreetmap.org

Morning: Start your day with horseback riding.

Afternoon: Have a refreshing lunch at Drift Bar.

Address: 50 meters South of Tropico Latino, Puntarenas Province, Santa teresa, 60111, Costa Rica

Evening: Go souvenir shopping in Santa Teresa and have coffee and cake at The Bakery.

The Bakery address: 30m north of Banco Nacional, Provincia de Puntarenas, santa teresa, 60111, Costa Rica

Day 10: A Relaxing Day in Playa Carmen

Morning: Take a refreshing yoga class on the sandy beaches of Playa del Carmen.

Afternoon: Have lunch and relax on the beach.

Evening: Shop, eat, and relax even more.

Day 11: Snorkeling in Playas del Coco

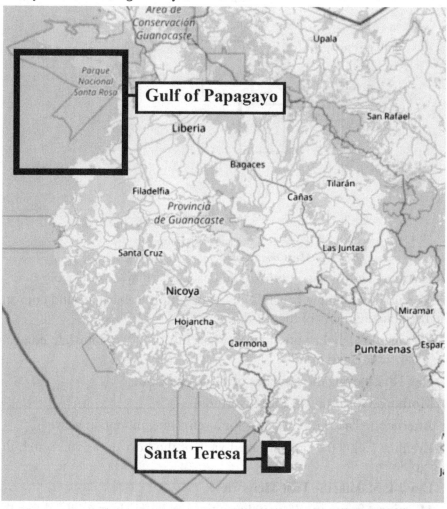

Gulf of Papagayo.
OpenStreetMap Contributors https://www.openstreetmap.org

Morning: Take a private boating tour around the Gulf of Papagayo, which offers snorkeling.

Afternoon/Evening: Enjoy a bit of downtime by the beach.

Day 12: Fishing and Beach Hopping

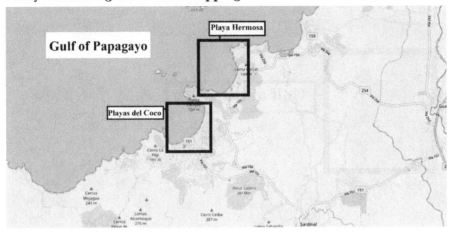

Playas del Coco and Playa Hermosa.
OpenStreetMap Contributors https://www.openstreetmap.org

Morning: Go fishing on one of the beaches at Playas del Coco.

Afternoon: Continue beach hopping or simply walking around enjoying the breathtaking views of the shoreline.

Evening: Watch the sunset from a beachfront restaurant while enjoying the local cuisine and drinks.

Day 13: Enjoying the Beaches of Playa Hermosa

Morning: Go surfing in Playa Hermosa.

Afternoon: Take an ATV tour for a refreshing mountain view.

Evening: Enjoy the unobstructed view of the horizon as you watch the sun go down.

Day 14: Making the Last Memories

Morning/Afternoon: If you have time, take a short walk along the nearby beaches to gather the last vacation memories before flying out of Guanacaste Airport.

Bonus Chapter: Useful Survival Phrases

Learning basic Costa Rican Spanish is valuable for you as a traveler, as it facilitates effective communication with the local population. While English is spoken in tourist hubs, many Costa Ricans converse in Spanish. Acquiring fundamental phrases enhances interactions, fostering a deeper understanding of the culture and enabling more meaningful connections with locals. Moreover, knowing basic Spanish proves practical for everyday scenarios like seeking directions, ordering food, and making purchases.

Knowing some phrases can help you form connections with locals.
https://unsplash.com/photos/text-R4sP8_Bq0Bw?utm_content=creditShareLink&utm_medium=referral&utm_source=unsplash

This linguistic capability becomes especially advantageous when exploring off-the-beaten-path areas where English proficiency may be limited. Your ability to communicate in Spanish is crucial for seeking assistance in emergencies or in unforeseen circumstances. Demonstrating respect for the local culture, your effort to learn the language contributes to a more immersive travel experience, allowing you to engage authentically with Costa Rican life. Overall, even a modest command of Costa Rican Spanish can enrich your travel experience, leading to more fulfilling and authentic encounters during your journey.

Phrases to Remember

Greetings
- **Hello** - Hola (oh-lah).
- **Hi** - ¡Hola! (ee-lah).
- **Good Morning** - Buenos días (bwehn-os dee-has).
- **Good Afternoon** - Buenas tardes (bwehn-as tar-des).
- **Good Evening/Night** - Buenas noches (bwehn-as noh-chess).
- **How Are You?** - Cómo estás (koh-mo es-tahs?).
- **What's Up?** - Qué tal (keh tahl?).
- **Nice to Meet You** - Mucho gusto (moo-choh goo-stoh).
- **How's It Going?** - Cómo va (koh-mo vah?).
- **Long Time No See** - Cuánto tiempo sin verte (kwahn-toh tee-em-poh seen vehr-teh).

Farewells
- **Goodbye** - Adiós (ah-dee-ohs).
- **See You Later** - Hasta luego (ahs-tah lweh-go).
- **See You Soon** - Hasta pronto (ahs-tah prohn-toh).
- **Until Next Time** - Hasta la próxima (ahs-tah lah prok-si-mah).
- **Take Care** - Cuídate (kwee-dah-teh).
- **Have a Good Day** - Que tengas un buen día (keh tehn-gas oon bwehn dee-ah).
- **Have a Good Trip** - Buen viaje (bwehn vyah-heh).
- **Farewell** - Despedida (dehs-peh-dee-dah).
- **Good Night** - Buenas noches (bwehn-as noh-chess).
- **Sweet Dreams** - Dulces sueños (dool-ses sweh-nyos).

Small Talk

- **What's Your Name?** - Cómo te llamas (koh-mo teh yah-mahs?).
- **Nice to Meet You.** - Mucho gusto (moo-choh goo-stoh).
- **How's the Day Treating You?** - Cómo te trata el día (koh-mo teh trah-tah el dee-ah?).
- **Lovely Weather Today, Isn't It?** - Lindo día hoy, verdad (leen-doh dee-ah oy, vehr-dah?).
- **Where Are You From?** - De dónde eres (deh dohn-deh eh-rehs?).
- **Have You Been Here Long?** - Has estado aquí mucho tiempo (ahs ehs-tah-doh ah-kee moo-choh tee-em-poh?).
- **What Do You Do for a Living?** - A qué te dedicas (ah keh teh deh-dee-kahs?).
- **Do You Have Any Recommendations for Things to Do Around Here?** - Tienes alguna recomendación para hacer por aquí (tye-nehs ahl-goo-nah reh-koh-men-dah-syon pah-rah ah-ser por ah-kee?).
- **Do You Know of Any Interesting Events Happening Nearby?** - Sabes de algún evento interesante cerca (sah-bes deh ahl-goon eh-vehn-toh een-teh-reh-san-te sehr-kah?).
- **Are There Any Local Customs or Traditions I Should Be Aware of?** - Hay costumbres o tradiciones locales de las que debería saber? (ai kohs-toom-bres o trah-dee-syon-es loh-kah-les de las keh de-beh-ree-ah sah-ber?).
- **What's Your Favorite Thing About This Place?** - Cuál es tu cosa favorita de este lugar? (kwahl es too koh-sah fah-boh-ree-tah deh ehs-teh loo-gahr?).
- **Do You Have Any Travel Tips for Someone New to the Area?** - Tienes algún consejo de viaje para alguien nuevo en la zona? (tye-nehs ahl-goon kohn-seh-hoh deh vyah-heh pah-rah ahl-gyen nweh-boh en lah soh-nah?).
- **What Languages Do You Speak?** - Qué idiomas hablas? (keh ee-dyoh-mahs ah-blahs?).
- **How's the Local Cuisine? Any Must-Try Dishes?** - Qué tal la comida local? ¿Hay algún plato que deba probar? (keh tahl lah koh-mee-dah loh-kahl? ai ahl-goon plah-toh keh deh-bah proh-

bahr?).

- **Have You Visited Any Nearby Attractions?** - Has visitado alguna atracción cercana? (ahs vee-si-tah-doh ahl-goo-nah ah-trahk-syon sehr-kah-nah?).
- **What's the Best Way to Get Around the City?** - Cuál es la mejor manera de moverse por la ciudad? (kwahl es lah meh-hor mah-neh-rah deh moh-vehr-se por lah syoo-dahd?).
- **Are There Any Local Markets or Shops Worth Exploring?** - Hay mercados o tiendas locales que valga la pena explorar? (ai mair-kah-dohs o tee-en-dahs loh-kah-les keh vahl-gah lah peh-nah ehk-sploh-rahr?).
- **Do You Have Any Favorite Spots for Outdoor Activities?** - Tienes lugares favoritos para actividades al aire libre? (tye-nehs loo-gah-res fah-boh-ree-tos pah-rah ahk-tee-vee-dah-dehs ahl ai-reh oh-bre?).
- **How's the Nightlife Around Here?** - Cómo es la vida nocturna por aquí? (koh-mo es lah vee-dah nohk-tur-nah por ah-kee?).
- **Is There a Local Tradition or Festival You Particularly Enjoy?** - Hay alguna tradición o festival local que disfrutes especialmente? (ai ahl-goo-nah trah-dee-syon o fes-tee-val loh-kahl keh dees-fru-tehs es-peh-syal-men-te?).
- **Can You Recommend a Good Place to Relax and Unwind?** - Puedes recomendar un buen lugar para relajarse? (pweh-dehs reh-koh-men-dar oon bwehn loo-gahr pah-rah reh-lah-hahr-se?).
- **What's Your Favorite Aspect of the Local Culture?** - Cuál es tu aspecto favorito de la cultura local? (kwahl es too ah-spehk-toh fah-boh-ree-toh deh lah kool-too-rah loh-kahl?).
- **Are There Any Local Artists or Musicians You Recommend Checking Out?** - Hay artistas o músicos locales que recomiendes conocer? (ai ar-tees-tahs o moo-see-kos loh-kah-les keh reh-koh-myen-des koh-noh-ser?).

Getting Around

- **How Do I Get to [Destination]?** - Cómo llego a [destino]? (koh-moh yeh-go ah [dees-tee-no]?).
- **Is There Public Transportation to [Place]?** - Hay transporte público a [lugar]? (ai trans-por-teh poo-blee-koh ah [loo-gar]?).

- **Where Can I Find a Taxi/Bus Station?** - Dónde puedo encontrar una parada de taxi/autobús? (dohn-deh pweh-doh en-kon-trar oo-nah pah-rah-dah deh tah-ksi/ow-toh-boos?).
- **How Much Is a Ticket to [Destination]?** - Cuánto cuesta un boleto a [destino]? (kwahn-toh kwes-tah oon boh-leh-toh ah [dees-tee-no]?).
- **Can You Recommend a Reliable Transportation Service?** - Puedes recomendar un servicio de transporte confiable? (pweh-dehs reh-koh-men-dar oon ser-bee-syo deh trans-por-teh kon-fee-ah-ble?).

Seeking Help

- **Can You Help Me?** - Puedes ayudarme? (pweh-dehs ah-yoo-dar-meh?).
- **Where Is the Nearest Pharmacy?** - Dónde está la farmacia más cercana? (dohn-deh ehs-tah lah far-mah-syah mahs sehr-kah-nah?).
- **Is There a Hospital Nearby?** - Hay un hospital cercano? (ai ohs-pee-tahl sehr-kah-no?).
- **Do You Speak English?** - Hablas inglés? (ah-blahs een-glehs?).
- **Can You Show Me on the Map?** - Puedes mostrarme en el mapa? (pweh-dehs mohs-trar-meh en el mah-pah?).

Eating Out

- **Is There a Good Restaurant Around Here?** - Hay un buen restaurante por aquí? (ai oon bwehn res-tau-ran-te por ah-kee?).
- **What's the Specialty of This Restaurant?** - Cuál es la especialidad de este restaurante? (kwahl es lah es-peh-syah-lee-dahd deh ehs-teh res-tau-ran-te?).
- **Can I See the Menu, Please?** - Puedo ver el menú, por favor? (pweh-doh ver el meh-noo, por fah-vor?).
- **Do You Have Vegetarian Options?** - Tienen opciones vegetarianas? (tye-nehn op-see-oh-nes veh-heh-tah-ree-ah-nas?).
- **Is Service Included in the Bill?** - Está incluido el servicio en la cuenta? (ehs-tah een-klee-doh el sehr-bee-syo en lah kwehn-tah?).

Medical Emergencies

- **I'm Not Feeling Well** - No me encuentro bien (noh meh en-kwon-troh byen).

- **Is There a Hospital Nearby?** - Hay un hospital cercano? (ai ohs-pee-tahl sehr-kah-no?).
- **I Need a Doctor** - Necesito un médico (neh-seh-see-toh oon meh-dee-ko).
- **Where Can I Find a Pharmacy?** - Dónde puedo encontrar una farmacia? (dohn-deh pweh-doh en-kon-trar oo-nah far-mah-syah?).

Lost or in Trouble

- **I'm Lost** - Estoy perdido/perdida (ehs-toy pehr-dee-doh/pehr-dee-dah).
- **Can You Help Me Find My Way Back?** - Puedes ayudarme a encontrar el camino de vuelta? (pweh-dehs ah-yoo-dar-meh ah en-kon-trar el kah-mee-no deh vwehl-tah?).
- **I've Been Robbed** - Me han robado (meh ahn roh-bah-doh).
- **I've Lost My [Documents/Wallet/Phone]** - He perdido mis [documentos / cartera / teléfono] (eh pehr-dee-doh mees [doh-koo-men-tos/kar-teh-rah/teh-leh-foh-no]).

Safety Concerns

- **Is It Safe Here?** - Es seguro aquí? (ehs seh-goo-ro ah-kee?).
- **I Feel Threatened** - Me siento amenazado/amenazada (meh syen-toh ah-meh-nah-sah-doh/ah-meh-nah-sah-dah).
- **Can You Call the Police?** - Puedes llamar a la policía? (pweh-dehs yah-mar ah lah poh-lee-see-ah?).

Communication Issues

- **I Don't Speak [the Language] Well** - No hablo bien [el idioma] (noh ah-bloh byen [el ee-dyoh-mah]).
- **Is There Someone Who Speaks English?** - Hay alguien que hable inglés? (ai ahl-gyen keh ah-bleh een-glehs?).

Common Words to Know

Numbers

- **One** - Uno (oo-noh).
- **Two** - Dos (dohs).
- **Three** - Tres (trehs).
- **Four** - Cuatro (kwah-troh).

- **Five** - Cinco (seen-koh).
- **Six** - Seis (seis).
- **Seven** - Siete (syeh-teh).
- **Eight** - Ocho (oh-cho).
- **Nine** - Nueve (nweh-veh).
- **Ten** - Diez (dyehs).

Days of the Week
- **Monday** - Lunes (loo-nes).
- **Tuesday** - Martes (mar-tes).
- **Wednesday** - Miércoles (myehr-koh-les).
- **Thursday** - Jueves (hweh-vehs).
- **Friday** - Viernes (vyer-nes).
- **Saturday** - Sábado (sah-bah-doh).
- **Sunday** - Domingo (doh-meen-goh).

Common Words
- **Hello** - Hola (oh-lah).
- **Goodbye** - Adiós (ah-dee-ohs).
- **Please** - Por favor (pohr fah-vohr).
- **Thank You** - Gracias (grah-see-ahs).
- **Excuse Me** - Perdón/Disculpe (pehr-dohn/dees-kool-peh).
- **Sorry** - Lo siento (loh see-ehn-toh).
- **Yes** - Sí (see).
- **No** - No (noh).
- **Maybe** - Tal vez (tal vehs).
- **I Don't Understand** - No entiendo (noh en-tee-ehn-doh).

Basic Questions
- **What?** - Qué? (keh).
- **Where?** - Dónde? (dohn-deh).
- **When?** - Cuándo? (kwan-doh).
- **How?** - Cómo? (koh-moh).
- **Why?** - Por qué? (por keh).
- **How Much?** - Cuánto/a? (kwahn-toh/toh).

- **Who?** - Quién? (kyen).
- **Which?** - Cuál? (kwahl).
- **Can I?** - Puedo? (pweh-doh).
- **Is There?** - Hay? (ai).

Directions
- **Left** - Izquierda (eez-kee-ehr-dah).
- **Right** - Derecha (deh-reh-chah).
- **Straight** - Derecho (deh-reh-cho).
- **North** - Norte (nor-teh).
- **South** - Sur (soor).
- **East** - Este (ehs-teh).
- **West** - Oeste (oh-es-teh).
- **Near** - Cerca (ser-kah).
- **Far** - Lejos (leh-hos).
- **Next to** - Al lado de (ahl lah-doh deh).

Time
- **Today** - Hoy (oy).
- **Tomorrow** - Mañana (mah-nyah-nah).
- **Yesterday** - Ayer (ah-yer).
- **Now** - Ahora (ah-o-rah).
- **Later** - Más tarde (mahs tar-deh).
- **Morning** - Mañana (mah-nyah-nah).
- **Afternoon** - Tarde (tar-deh).
- **Evening/Night** - Noche (noh-che).
- **Hour** - Hora (oh-rah).
- **Minute** - Minuto (mee-noo-toh).

Eating Out
- **Food** - Comida (koh-mee-dah).
- **Water** - Agua (ah-gwah).
- **Menu** - Menú (meh-noo).
- **Breakfast** - Desayuno (deh-sah-yoo-no).
- **Lunch** - Almuerzo (ahl-mwehr-so).

- **Dinner** - Cena (seh-nah).
- **Coffee** - Café (kah-feh).
- **Tea** - Té (teh).
- **Bill/Check** - Cuenta (kwehn-tah).
- **Tasty/Delicious** - Sabroso/a (sah-broh-soh/sah-broh-sah).

Shopping
- **Market** - Mercado (mehr-kah-doh).
- **Shop/Store** - Tienda (tyen-dah).
- **Money** - Dinero (dee-neh-ro).
- **How Much Does It Cost?** - Cuánto cuesta? (kwahn-toh kwes-tah).
- **Expensive** - Caro/a (kah-roh/kah-rah).
- **Cheap** - Barato/a (bah-rah-toh/bah-rah-tah).
- **Sale** - Rebaja (reh-bah-ha).
- **Size** - Tamaño (ta-mahn-yo).
- **Color** - Color (koh-lor).
- **I Want to Buy...** - Quiero comprar... (kyeh-roh kohm-prar).

Transportation
- **Bus** - Autobús (ow-toh-boos).
- **Train** - Tren (trehn).
- **Taxi** - Taxi (tah-ksee).
- **Airport** - Aeropuerto (ah-eh-roh-pwehr-toh).
- **Ticket** - Boleto (boh-leh-toh).
- **Car** - Coche (koh-cheh).
- **Bicycle** - Bicicleta (bee-thee-kleh-tah).
- **Subway/Metro** - Metro (meh-troh).
- **Stop** - Parada (pah-rah-dah).
- **Go** - Ir (eer).

Accommodation
- **Hotel** - Hotel (oh-tehl).
- **Room** - Habitación (ah-bee-tah-syon).
- **Reservation** - Reserva (reh-ser-vah).
- **Check-in** - Registro de entrada (reh-hees-troh deh en-trah-dah).

- **Check-out** - Registro de salida (reh-hees-troh deh sah-lee-dah).
- **Key** - Llave (yah-veh).
- **Wi-Fi** - Wi-Fi (wee-fee).
- **Towel** - Toalla (toh-ah-yah).
- **Bed** - Cama (kah-mah).
- **Pillow** - Almohada (ahl-mo-ah-dah).

Health and Safety
- **Doctor** - Médico (meh-dee-koh).
- **Pharmacy** - Farmacia (far-mah-syah).
- **Hospital** - Hospital (ohs-pee-tahl).
- **Medicine** - Medicina (meh-dee-see-nah).
- **Emergency** - Emergencia (eh-mehr-hen-syah).
- **Police** - Policía (poh-lee-see-ah).
- **Fire** - Fuego (fweh-go).
- **Help** - Ayuda (ah-yoo-dah).
- **Injured** - Herido/a (eh-ree-doh/ah).
- **Safe** - Seguro/a (seh-goo-ro/seh-goo-rah).

Feel free to use this list as a reference during your travels. Learning these common words will help you communicate effectively and navigate various situations in a foreign country.

Appendix

This appendix section includes an A to Z list of all attractions, monuments, museums, etc, mentioned throughout the book.

- Arenal Volcano, La Fortuna, Alajuela - Mentioned in Chapter 5.
- Avenida Escazú, San José - Mentioned in Chapter 3.
- Atenas, Alajuela - Mentioned in Chapter 5.
- Alberto Manuel Brenes Biological Reserve, San Ramón, Alajuela - Mentioned in Chapter 5.
- Alajuela Cathedral, Alajuela - Mentioned in Chapter 5.
- Bay of Salinas, Guanacaste- Mentioned in Chapter 6.
- Barva, Cartago, and Heredia - Mentioned in Chapter 7.
- Basilica of Our Lady of the Angel, Cartago, and Heredia - Mentioned in Chapter 7.
- Britt Coffee tour in Heredia, San José - Mentioned in Chapter 3.
- Cachi Dam, Orosi, Cartago, and Heredia - Mentioned in Chapter 7.
- Cacao Trails, The Caribbean Coast (Limon Province) - Mentioned in Chapter 8.
- Cathedral of Alajuela, Alajuela - Mentioned in Chapter 5.
- Central Park, San José - Mentioned in Chapter 3.
- Children's Museum, San José - Mentioned in Chapter 3.
- Central Park (Parque Central), Alajuela - Mentioned in Chapter5.

- Cahuita National Park, The Caribbean Coast (Limon Province) - Mentioned in Chapter 8.
- Colonial San José de Orosi Church, Cartago, and Heredia - Mentioned in Chapter 7.
- Cabo Blanco Natural Reserve, Puntarenas - Mentioned in Chapter 4.
- Diamante Eco Adventure Park, Guanacaste - Mentioned in Chapter 6.
- El FortínCartago and Heredia - Mentioned in Chapter 7.
- Finca La Isla Botanical Garden, The Caribbean Coast (Limon Province) - Mentioned in Chapter 8.
- Grecia, Alajuela - Mentioned in Chapter 5.
- General Tomas Guardia Park, Alajuela - Mentioned in Chapter 5.
- Gold Museum, San José - Mentioned in Chapter 3.
- Guanacaste Conservation Area, Guanacaste - Mentioned in Chapter 6.
- Guayabo National Monument, Cartago, and Heredia - Mentioned in Chapter 7.
- Gandoca-Manzanillo Wildlife Refuge, The Caribbean Coast (Limon Province) - Mentioned in Chapter 8.
- Iglesia de Grecia (Metal Church), Village of Grecia, Alajuela - Mentioned in Chapter 5.
- Iglesia de San Jose De Orosi Church, Orosi, Cartago, and Heredia - Mentioned in Chapter 7.
- Jaco Horseback Riding, Puntarenas - Mentioned in Chapter 4.
- Juan Santamaria Monument, Alajuela - Mentioned in Chapter 5.
- Liberia, Guanacaste - Mentioned in Chapter 6.
- La Paz Waterfall Gardens, San José - Mentioned in Chapter 3.
- Los Chorros Municipal Recreational Park - Mentioned in Chapter 5.
- La Selva Biological Station, Sarapiqui, Cartago, and Heredia - Mentioned in Chapter 7.
- Llanos de Cortez Waterfall, Guanacaste - Mentioned in Chapter 6.

- Luluberlu Art Gallery, The Caribbean Coast (Limon Province) - Mentioned in Chapter 8.
- La Ceiba Reserve, The Caribbean Coast (Limon Province) - Mentioned in Chapter 8.
- La Fortuna, Alajuela - Mentioned in Chapter 5.
- Manuel Antonio National Park, San José - Mentioned in Chapter 3.
- Montezuma Waterfalls, Puntarenas - Mentioned in Chapter 4.
- Monkey Park, Tamarindo, Guanacaste - Mentioned in Chapter 6.
- Monteverde Cloud Forest Reserve, Puntarenas - Mentioned in Chapter 4.
- Manuel Antonio National Park, Puntarenas - Mentioned in Chapter 4.
- Metal Church (Iglesia de Grecia, Alajuela - Mentioned in Chapter 5.
- Museum of Cultures, Cartago, and Heredia - Mentioned in Chapter 7.
- Malecón, The Caribbean Coast (Limon Province) - Mentioned in Chapter 8.
- Manzanillo Beach, The Caribbean Coast (Limon Province) - Mentioned in Chapter 8.
- Museo Histórico Cultural Juan Santamaría, Alajuela - Mentioned in Chapter 5.
- National University of Costa Rica, Cartago, and Heredia - Mentioned in Chapter 7.
- National Biodiversity Institute of Costa Rica (INBioparque), Cartago and Heredia - Mentioned in Chapter 7.
- National Theatre, San José - Mentioned in Chapter 3.
- NATUWA Wildlife Sanctuary, Puntarenas - Mentioned in Chapter 4.
- Ostional Wildlife Refuge, Guanacaste - Mentioned in Chapter 6.
- Pre-Columbian Gold Museum, San José - Mentioned in Chapter 3.
- Plaza Real Cariari, San José - Mentioned in Chapter 3.
- Poas Volcano, Alajuela - Mentioned in Chapter 5.

- Parque Diversiones, San José - Mentioned in Chapter 3.
- Parque Marino del Pacifico, Puntarenas - Mentioned in Chapter 4.
- Palo Verde National Park, Guanacaste- Mentioned in Chapter 6.
- Playa Puerto Viejo, The Caribbean Coast (Limon Province) - Mentioned in Chapter 8.
- Playa Guiones, Guanacaste- Mentioned in Chapter 6.
- Playa Flamingo, Guanacaste- Mentioned in Chapter 6.
- Playa Conchal, Guanacaste- Mentioned in Chapter 6.
- Pargas Vargas - Mentioned in Chapter 8.
- Playa Chiquita Beach, The Caribbean Coast (Limon Province) - Mentioned in Chapter 8.
- Punta Uva beach, The Caribbean Coast (Limon Province) - Mentioned in Chapter 8.
- Puerto Limón, The Caribbean Coast (Limon Province) - Mentioned in Chapter 8.
- Puerto Viejo de Sarapiquí, Cartago and Heredia - Mentioned in Chapter 7.
- Rescate Wildlife Rescue Center, San José - Mentioned in Chapter 3.
- Rio Celeste waterfall, San José - Mentioned in Chapter 3.
- Rincon de la Vieja National Park, Guanacaste- Mentioned in Chapter 6.
- San Ramón, Alajuela - Mentioned in Chapter 5.
- Sarchí, Alajuela - Mentioned in Chapter 5.
- Santa Rosa National Park and Guanacaste National Park, Guanacaste- Mentioned in Chapter 6.
- Santo Domingo, Cartago, and Heredia - Mentioned in Chapter 7.
- Simon Bolivar Zoo, San José - Mentioned in Chapter 3.
- Santa Teresa Beach, Puntarenas - Mentioned in Chapter 4.
- Tortuguero National Park, San José - Mentioned in Chapter 3.
- Tortuguero National Park, San José - Mentioned in Chapter 3.
- Tarcoles Crocodile Bridge, Jaco City, Puntarenas - Mentioned in

Chapter 4.
- The Hanging Bridge Tour, Puntarenas - Mentioned in Chapter 4.
- Topiary garden - Mentioned in Chapter 5.
- Tamarindo Beach, Guanacaste- Mentioned in Chapter 6.
- The ruins of Santiago Apóstol ParishCartago and Heredia - Mentioned in Chapter 7.
- Tortuguero National Park, The Caribbean Coast (Limon Province) - Mentioned in Chapter 8.
- Tortuguero Beach, The Caribbean Coast (Limon Province) - Mentioned in Chapter 8.
- Talamanca Viewpoint, The Caribbean Coast (Limon Province) - Mentioned in Chapter 8.
- The Sixaola Bridge, The Caribbean Coast (Limon Province) - Mentioned in Chapter 8.
- Turrialba, Cartago, and Heredia - Mentioned in Chapter 7.
- Zarcero, Alajuela - Mentioned in Chapter 5.

Conclusion

This guidebook has introduced you to Costa Rica, the land of tropical rainforests, green mountains, coffee plantations, and many tourist attractions. Named by Christopher Columbus in 1502, the "rich coast" has come a long way since its foundations. From the first chapter, you've gotten to know Costa Rica, including its geographical location, regions, and counties, founding and background history, how it relates to the other Central American countries, interesting facts about its culture, cuisine, art, crafts, customs, transportation, and everything else you need to know before visiting the country. The second chapter offered useful information on navigating travel to and from Costa Rica airports, including the main one, Juan Santamaría International Airport (SJO).

The subsequent chapters guided you through Costa Rica's main regions, beginning with San Jose, the capital district. Beyond exploring the region's natural beauties through organized tours (including the rainforest area and wildlife habitats surrounding San Jose), you were also encouraged to learn about the local culture through authentic experiences. Next, you were taken on a tour of Puntarenas Province through the picturesque beaches of Montezuma, the great waves of Santa Teresa, the lush forests of Mal País, and more. Chapter Five showcased Alajuela, another Costa Rican province known for its variety of attractions, natural landscapes (like the famous La Fortuna), and cultural highlights. Similarly, the next chapters introduced Guanacaste, Cartago, and Heredia regions, and the Limón Province, taking you through journeys offering a mix of adventure and relaxation, historical insights, and cultural richness boasting Latin and unique Afro-Caribbean influences.

To provide even more guidance for which sights to visit when traveling to Costa Rica, chapter nine brought you comprehensive thematic and traveler-oriented itineraries and programs, along with maps that display the routes you propose. If you have an idea of which places you want to visit, you can always modify the programs, but if you don't, they will act as a helping hand when planning your dream Costa Rican vacation.

Since many Costa Ricans speak only Spanish and indigenous languages, learning a few Spanish phrases is a good way to get around and immerse yourself safely in local life and culture. Feel free to refer to the useful survival phrases provided in the bonus chapter of this book to learn to communicate effectively with the locals. Lastly, the book provides a cheat sheet for all the wonderful sights to see in Costa Rica, which are mentioned throughout the book and can serve as an initial guide to decide where to head when visiting the country. Now that you have all this useful information about Costa Rica, you can start planning your dream vacation.

If you enjoyed this book, a review on Amazon would be greatly appreciated because it would mean a lot to hear from you.

To leave a review:
1. Open your camera app.
2. Point your mobile device at the QR code.
3. The review page will appear in your web browser.

Thanks for your support!

Here's another book by Captivating Travels that you might like

Welcome Aboard, Discover Your Limited-Time Free Bonus!

Hello, traveler! Welcome to the Captivating Travels family, and thanks for grabbing a copy of this book! Since you've chosen to join us on this journey, we'd like to offer you something special.

Check out the link below for a FREE Ultimate Travel Checklist eBook & Printable PDF to make your travel planning stress-free and enjoyable.

But that's not all - you'll also gain access to our exclusive email list with even more free e-books and insider travel tips. Well, what are you waiting for? Click the link below to join and embark on your next adventure with ease.

Access your bonus here:
https://livetolearn.lpages.co/checklist/
Or, Scan the QR code!

References

Aldi, C. (2022, July 13). 13 Top Festivals in Costa Rica - Special Places of Costa Rica. Special Places of Costa Rica. https://www.specialplacesofcostarica.com/blog/festivals-in-costa-rica/

Aldi, C. (2023, August 23). 4 Popular Sports in Costa Rica. Special Places of Costa Rica. https://www.specialplacesofcostarica.com/blog/sports-in-costa-rica/

Altair Souvenir & Gallery Shop - All You Need to Know BEFORE You Go (with Photos). (n.d.). Trip Advisor. https://www.tripadvisor.com/Attraction_Review-g309289-d10021221-Reviews-Altair_Souvenir_Gallery_Shop-Quepos_Province_of_Puntarenas.html

Andrey, S. (2017, September 12). Information & Facts about the Puntarenas Province, Costa Rica. Go Tours Costa Rica. https://gotourscostarica.com/blog/puntarenas-province

Araya, J. (2020a, October 30). Turrialba Costa Rica Travel Guide. Travel Excellence. https://www.travelexcellence.com/blog/turrialba-costa-rica-travel-guide/

Araya, J. (2020b, November 3). Sarapiquí Costa Rica Travel Guide. Travel Excellence. https://www.travelexcellence.com/blog/sarapiqui-costa-rica-travel-guide/

Barva, Costa Rica - City Guide. (n.d.). Go Visit Costa Rica. https://www.govisitcostarica.com/region/city.asp?cID=217

Barva, Costa Rica 2024: Best Places to Visit. (n.d.). Trip Advisor. https://www.tripadvisor.com/Tourism-g309255-Barva_Province_of_Heredia-Vacations.html

BBC News. (2018, May 10). Costa Rica Country Profile. BBC News. https://www.bbc.com/news/world-latin-america-19414068

Beachtown Travel. (2023, February 18). An Introduction to the Seven Provinces of Costa Rica. Beachtowntravel.com. https://theblog.beachtowntravel.com/an-introduction-to-the-seven-provinces-of-costa-rica

Broad, D. (n.d.). Basilica of Our Lady of the Angels, Cartago. City Seeker. https://cityseeker.com/san-jose/198185-basilica-of-our-lady-of-the-angels

Cartago Ruins. (n.d.). Tourism in Costa Rica. https://www.tourismincostarica.org/cartago-ruins#:~:text=Cartago%20Ruins%2C%20also%20known%20as

Cartago, Costa Rica. (n.d.). Tourism in Costa Rica. https://www.tourismincostarica.org/cartago

CLARO QUE SI SEAFOOD RESTAURANT, Manuel Antonio - Menu, Prices & Restaurant Reviews. (n.d.). Trip Advisor. https://www.tripadvisor.com/Restaurant_Review-g309274-d1234080-Reviews-Claro_Que_Si_Seafood_Restaurant-Manuel_Antonio_Quepos_Province_of_Puntarenas.html

Costa Rica Activities. (2019). Go Visit Costa Rica. https://www.govisitcostarica.com/activities.asp

Costa Rica Culture: Language, Religion, Food. (n.d.). Original Travel. https://www.originaltravel.co.uk/travel-guide/costa-rica/culture

Costa Rica Indigenous Art and Crafts. (2024). Costa Rican Vacations. https://www.vacationscostarica.com/places-to-visit/local-communities/

Costa Rica Regions. (n.d.). Costa Rica Guides. https://www.costaricaguides.com/costa_rica_regions/

Costa Rica Second Most Peaceful Country in Latin America. (n.d.). Travel Excellence. https://www.travelexcellence.com/latest-news/costa-rica-second-most-peaceful-country-in-latin-america/

Costa Rica Tourism Board. (2019). Visit Costa Rica. Visit Costa Rica. https://www.visitcostarica.com/en

Costa Rica Travel Life. (2022a, February 1). 13 Fun Things to do in Alajuela, Costa Rica. Costa Rica Travel Life. https://costaricatravellife.com/alajuela-costa-rica/

Costa Rica Travel Life. (2022b, March 24). 11 BEST Restaurants in San Jose, Costa Rica. Costa Rica Travel Life. https://costaricatravellife.com/restaurants-in-san-jose-costa-rica/

Costa Rica Travel Life. (2022c, June 10). Ultimate Guide to Guanacaste, Costa Rica, and Fun Things to Do. Costa Rica Travel Life. https://costaricatravellife.com/guanacaste-costa-rica-guide/

Costa Rica Travel Life. (2022d, August 16). 21 Things to KNOW Before Visiting Cahuita National Park. Costa Rica Travel Life. https://costaricatravellife.com/cahuita-national-park/

Costa Rica Travel Life. (2022e, December 27). 12 BEST Things to do in Puntarenas, Costa Rica. Costa Rica Travel Life. https://costaricatravellife.com/puntarenas-costa-rica/

Costa Rica Trip. (2022, January 16). Best Coffee Tours in Costa Rica - Coffee Plantation Tours. Costa Rica Trip | Travel Guide. https://costarica-trip.com/tours/coffee-tours-in-costa-rica/

Costa Rica. (n.d.). Cahuita Getting Around. Costa Rica. https://www.costarica.com/destinations/cahuita/getting-around

Costa Rican Wildlife Introduction. A Visit to the Zoo. Private Tour. (n.d.). Viator. https://www.viator.com/San-Jose/d793-ttd/p-26853P83?pid=P00057689&mcid=42383&medium=link&campaign=while-in-costa-rica

CostaRica.org | Your Guide to Costa Rican Vacations, Hotels, and Tours. (2018). Costa Rica. https://costarica.org/

Cultural Tourist Guide. (n.d.). https://www.ict.go.cr/flipbook/guias/PDF-en/GUIA_PUNTARENAS.pdf

Day Translations. (2013, October 23). Costa Rica. Day Translations Blog. https://www.daytranslations.com/blog/guide/costa-rica/5/

Departure Private Transfer: Puntarenas to San Jose Airport SJO by Minivan. (n.d.). Viator. https://www.viator.com/tours/Puntarenas/Departure-Private-Transfer-Puntarenas-to-San-Jose-Airport-SJO-by-Minivan/d4506-40380P334

Destinationless Travel. (2020, July 1). Cahuita National Park, Costa Rica - Everything You NEED To Know! Destinationless Travel. https://destinationlesstravel.com/cahuita-national-park-costa-rica/

Essential Costa Rica. (2016a, January 6). About Costa Rica. Visit Costa Rica. https://www.visitcostarica.com/en/costa-rica/general-information

Essential Costa Rica. (n.d.-a). Heredia Province. Visit Costa Rica. https://www.visitcostarica.com/en/costa-rica/knowing-costa-rica/heredia

Essential Costa Rica. (n.d.-b). Historical Walks through Cartago. Visit Costa Rica. https://www.visitcostarica.com/en/costa-rica/things-to-do/culture/historical-walks/cartago

Farley, S. (2014, November 11). Drive, Fly, or Take a Boat to Get to Santa Teresa, Costa Rica. Enchanting Costa Rica. https://enchanting-costarica.com/family-vacations/best-ways-get-santa-teresa-costa-rica/

Fly to/from the San José International Airport. (n.d.). Go Visit Costa Rica. https://www.govisitcostarica.com/region/city.asp?cID=407

García, M. (2021, September 11). 15 Things You Didn't Know About Santa Teresa, Costa Rica. Yoko Village. https://yokovillage.com/15-things-you-didnt-know-about-santa-teresa-costa-rica/

Garrigues, R. (n.d.). Alajuela, Costa Rica. Angel Fire. https://www.angelfire.com/bc/gonebirding/alajuela.html

Getting Around Costa Rica. (n.d.). US News. https://travel.usnews.com/Costa_Rica/Getting_Around/

Getting Around in Alajuela, Costa Rica. (n.d.). Go Visit Costa Rica. https://www.govisitcostarica.com/category/transportation/transportation.asp?rID=1

Guest Surf Blogger. (2015, March 7). Fun and Fantastical Facts about San Jose in Costa Rica. Shaka Costa Rica. https://www.shakacostarica.com/blog/fun-and-fantastical-facts-about-san-jose-in-costa-rica

Guide to Public Transportation in Costa Rica. (2023). Vacations Costa Rica. https://www.vacationscostarica.com/travel/public-transportation/

Heredia Costa Rica - A Small Mountain Town Near San Jose, Costa Rica. (n.d.). Costa Rica. https://costarica.org/cities/heredia/

Heredia, Costa Rica - City Guide. (n.d.). Go Visit Costa Rica. https://www.govisitcostarica.com/region/city.asp?cID=222

Heredia, Costa Rica: Where to Go & Things to Do. (n.d.). Costa Rica Escapes. https://www.creescapes.com/where-to-go-in-costa-rica/heredia/

Historic Costa Rica – Your Guide to the Ruins of Cartago. (2020, November 10). Costa Rica Rios. https://www.costaricarios.com/historic-costa-rica-your-guide-to-the-ruins-of-cartago/

Hotel Cayuga. (n.d.). Cayuga Hotel. Hotel Cayuga. https://hotelcayuga.com/en/

HOTEL LA PUNTA - Reviews (Puntarenas, Costa Rica). (n.d.). Trip Advisor. https://www.tripadvisor.com/Hotel_Review-g309287-d300838-Reviews-Hotel_La_Punta-Puntarenas_Province_of_Puntarenas.html

How to Get to Monteverde Cloud Forest Reserve. (n.d.). Horizon Guides. https://horizonguides.com/guides/costa-rica-national-parks/monteverde-cloud-forest-reserve

International Living. (2021, August 5). Limón Province, Costa Rica: Retirement Info and Cost of Living Budget - IL. International Living. https://internationalliving.com/countries/costa-rica/limon-province-costa-rica/

Isenberg, R. (2023, April 4). Getting Around in San José, Costa Rica. Lonely Planet. https://www.lonelyplanet.com/articles/getting-around-san-jose-costa-rica

Jaco Horseback Riding Adventure Tours. (n.d.). Viator. https://viator.com/tours/Jaco/Horseback-Riding-Tour/d4144-416848P1

Javi the Frog. (2013, February 22). Journey Back through Time on a Tour of Cartago's Ruins. Go Visit Costa Rica. https://www.govisitcostarica.com/blog/post/visit-ruins-cartago.aspx

Jenn and Matt. (2016, May 11). Montezuma Waterfalls: Best Ways to Access. Two Weeks in Costa Rica. https://www.twoweeksincostarica.com/montezuma-waterfalls/

Jenn and Matt. (2021, February 12). Santa Teresa: Costa Rica's Trending Beach Town. Two Weeks in Costa Rica. https://www.twoweeksincostarica.com/santa-teresa/

Jenn and Matt. (2023, July 8). Heredia, Costa Rica: City Guide. Two Weeks in Costa Rica. https://www.twoweeksincostarica.com/heredia-city-guide/

Jessica. (2021, January 6). The Ultimate Travel Guide to Guanacaste, Costa Rica. Bon Traveler. https://www.bontraveler.com/a-first-timers-guide-to-guanacaste-costa-rica/

Jungle Avenue - All You Need to Know BEFORE You Go (with Photos). (n.d.). Trip Advisor. https://www.tripadvisor.com/Attraction_Review-g309289-d1997501-Reviews-Jungle_Avenue-Quepos_Province_of_Puntarenas.html

Kong, S. L. (2020, October 26). 5 wild facts about Costa Rica's Manuel Antonio National Park. G Adventures Blog. https://www.gadventures.com/blog/manuel-antonio-costa-rica/

Kroeger, T. (2013, November 4). Discover the Ruins of Cartago - Santiago Apostol Parish. Universal Traveller. https://www.universal-traveller.com/ruins-of-the-temple-of-the-santiago-apostol-parish/

Kulluk, M. (2023, March 22). 14 Epic Things to do in Cahuita, Costa Rica. Peter Pan Traveler. https://www.peterpantraveler.com/things-to-do-in-cahuita/

LA JUNTA DOMINICAL - Menu, Prices & Restaurant Reviews. (n.d.). Trip Advisor. https://www.tripadvisor.com/Restaurant_Review-g313829-d23574319-Reviews-La_Junta_Dominical-Dominical_Province_of_Puntarenas.html

Liberia Guanacaste Airport (LIR). (2020, July 15). LIR Airport. https://www.lirairport.com/

Limon Domestic Airport, Costa Rica - City Guide. (n.d.). Go Visit Costa Rica. https://www.govisitcostarica.com/region/city.asp?cID=412

Llama Travel. (n.d.). About San Jose | History & Landmarks | Costa Rica. Llama Travel. https://www.llamatravel.com/destinations/latin-america/costa-rica/san-jose

Manuel Antonio National Park. (2014). Sinac. https://www.sinac.go.cr/EN-

US/ac/acopac/pnma/Pages/default.aspx

Manzanillo. (2023, November 3). Costa Rica. https://www.costarica.com/manzanillo/

McCloskey, T. (2018, January 31). 11 Facts about Costa Rica That Will Surprise You. Visit Costa Rica. https://www.visitcostarica.com/en/costa-rica/blog/11-facts-about-costa-rica-will-surprise-you

Monirul. (2014, March 9). Arts and Culture of Costa Rica. Costa Rica Journeys. https://www.costaricajourneys.com/arts-of-costa-rica/

Monteverde Costa Rica - Monteverde's Cloud Forest. (2000). Monteverde Info. https://www.monteverdeinfo.com/cloud-forests

Orosi River Valley - All You Need to Know BEFORE You Go (with Photos). (n.d.). Trip Advisor. https://www.tripadvisor.com/Attraction_Review-g309232-d592803-Reviews-Orosi_River_Valley-Orosi_Province_of_Cartago.html

Orosi Valley of Costa Rica - An Off-the-Beaten Path Destination. (n.d.). Costa Rica. https://costarica.org/cities/orosi-valley/

Orosi, Costa Rica - City Guide. (n.d.). Go Visit Costa Rica. https://www.govisitcostarica.com/region/city.asp?cID=197

OTG Team. (2018, March 19). Ten Interesting Facts about Costa Rica's Cloud Forests. On the Go Tours. https://www.onthegotours.com/blog/2018/03/facts-about-costa-ricas-cloud-forests/

Pacific Trade Winds. (2018). Basilica of Our Lady of Angels, Costa Rica. Enter Costa Rica. https://www.entercostarica.com/attractions/hidden-treasures/basilica-of-our-lady-of-angels

Palmares, Costa Rica - City Guide. (n.d.). Go Visit Costa Rica. https://www.govisitcostarica.com/region/city.asp?cID=102

Pavas International Airport (Tobías Bolaños), Costa Rica - City Guide. (n.d.). Go Visit Costa Rica. https://www.govisitcostarica.com/region/city.asp?cID=425

POSADA NATURA - Prices & Villa Reviews (Puntarenas, Costa Rica). (n.d.). Trip Advisor. https://www.tripadvisor.com/Hotel_Review-g309287-d2557609-Reviews-Posada_Natura-Puntarenas_Province_of_Puntarenas.html

Private Natural History Walk by Pasión Costa Rica. (n.d.). Viator. https://www.viator.com/tours/Puntarenas/Private-Monteverde-Cloud-Forest-Walk/d4506-33091P1

Puntarenas Costa Rica, Largest province, and Important Port City. (n.d.). Costa Rica. https://costarica.org/cities/puntarenas/

Puntarenas History Facts and Timeline: Puntarenas, Costa Rica. (2019, July 9). World Guides. http://www.world-guides.com/latin-america/costa-rica/puntarenas/puntarenas_history.html

Puntarenas Province Facts for Kids. (2023, November 26). Kiddle. https://kids.kiddle.co/Puntarenas_Province

Puntarenas Province, Costa Rica. (n.d.). Costa Rica Guides. https://www.costaricaguides.com/articles/provinces/puntarenas.html

Rica, C. (n.d.). Cartago, Costa Rica - So much history in one city, including the basilica. Costa Rica. https://costarica.org/cities/cartago/

RICO TICO JUNGLE GRILL, Manuel Antonio - Menu, Prices & Restaurant Reviews. (n.d.). Trip Advisor. https://www.tripadvisor.com/Restaurant_Review-g309274-d2062464-Reviews-Rico_Tico_Jungle_Grill-Manuel_Antonio_Quepos_Province_of_Puntarenas.html

Rico Tico Restaurant, Bar & Grill | Manuel Antonio, Costa Rica. (n.d.). Si Como No Resort. https://sicomono.com/en/rico-tico-restaurant-bar-grill-manuel-antonio/

Rodrick, S. (2023, August 31). How to Visit Montezuma Waterfalls, Costa Rica (For Free!). Sally Sees. https://sallysees.com/montezuma-waterfalls/

Sabrina & Andreas. (2019, December 26). Tortuguero National Park - Everything You Need to Know. Roads and Rivers. https://roads-and-rivers.com/en/tortuguero-national-park-costa-rica/

Sammi. (2020, November 11). Things to Do in San Jose, Costa Rica: Maps, Itineraries, Day Trips, Museums and more. My Tan Feet. https://mytanfeet.com/activities/things-to-do-in-san-jose-costa-rica/

Sammi. (2021, November 18). The Costa Rica Crocodile Bridge: the Famous Tarcoles River. My Tan Feet. https://mytanfeet.com/activities/rio-tarcoles-crocodiles-costa-rica/

Sammi. (2022, September 5). Rainforest Adventures Costa Rica Atlantic: Caribbean Adventure Park and Ecology Tours. My Tan Feet. https://mytanfeet.com/activities/rainforest-adventures-costa-rica-atlantic/

San Jose Juan Santamaria International Airport Profile | CAPA. (n.d.). Centre for Aviation. https://centreforaviation.com/data/profiles/airports/san-jose-juan-santamaria-international-airport-sjo

San Jose, Costa Rica. (n.d.). Costa Rica Guides. https://www.costaricaguides.com/costa_rica_regions/san_jose.html

Santo Domingo de Heredia, Costa Rica - City Guide. (n.d.). Go Visit Costa Rica. https://www.govisitcostarica.com/region/city.asp?cID=221

Sarapiqui in Costa Rica, Little Adventure in the Rainforest. (n.d.). Costa Rica. https://costarica.org/cities/sarapiqui/

Selvatura Park Hanging Bridge Canopy Tour in Monteverde. (n.d.). Viator. https://www.viator.com/tours/Monteverde/Hangin-Bridges/d24783-36710P3

Shared Shuttle Monteverde to Manuel Antonio. (n.d.). Viator. https://www.viator.com/tours/Puntarenas/Shared-shuttle-from-Arenal-to-Monteverde/d4506-113328P37

Surf Camp Costa Rica, Santa Teresa. (n.d.). Lapoint. https://lapointcamps.com/surfcamp/costa-rica/

THE 15 BEST Things to Do in Orosi - 2024 (with Photos). (n.d.). Trip Advisor. https://www.tripadvisor.com/Attractions-g309232-Activities-Orosi_Province_of_Cartago.html

The Explorer's Passage. (2023, July 3). Ultimate Guanacaste Travel Guide - Explore

Costa Rica's Coastal Paradise. The Explorer's Passage.
https://explorerspassage.com/chronicles/guanacaste-costa-rica/

The Mighty Barva Volcano. (n.d.). Go Visit Costa Rica.
https://www.govisitcostarica.com/travelInfo/volcanoes/barva-volcano.asp

Things to Do in Manuel Antonio National Park. (2000). Costa Rica Experts.
https://costaricaexperts.com/destinations/manuel-antonio/

Thomas, & Sarah. (2023, July 9). Manzanillo, Costa Rica: Idealic Caribbean Coast Beach Village. Costa Rica Vibes.
https://www.costaricavibes.com/destinations/caribbean/manzanillo/

Tico Pod Art House & Gifts - All You Need to Know BEFORE You Go (with Photos). (n.d.). Trip Advisor. https://www.tripadvisor.com/Attraction_Review-g309271-d3849926-Reviews-Tico_Pod_Art_House_Gifts-Jaco_Jaco_District_Garabito_Municipality_Province_of_Pun.html

Todd. (n.d.). Cartago, Costa Rica - City Guide. Go Visit Costa Rica.
https://www.govisitcostarica.com/region/city.asp?cID=201

Trad, M. (2017, September 18). Santo Domingo de Heredia, paradise on Earth. Don Quijote. https://www.donquijote.org/blog/santo-domingo-de-heredia-paradise-on-earth/

Travel Smart Ltd. (2019, September 7). Puerto Limon History Facts and Timeline: Puerto Limon, Costa Rica. Www.world-Guides.com. http://www.world-guides.com/latin-america/costa-rica/limon/puerto-limon/puerto_limon_history.html

Traveling Camera. (2019, July). Basilica of Los Angeles - Most Beautiful Place to Explore in Cartago, Costa Rica. Traveling Camera.
https://www.travellingcamera.com/2019/07/basilica-of-los-angeles-cartago-costa-rica.html

Tripadvisor LLC. (2021). Things to Do in Puerto Limon. Tripadvisor.
https://www.tripadvisor.com/Attractions-g309264-Activities-Puerto_Limon_Province_of_Limon.html

Tripadvisor LLC. (n.d.). THE 15 BEST Things to Do in Cahuita - 2024 (with Photos). Tripadvisor. https://www.tripadvisor.com/Attractions-g309262-Activities-Cahuita_Province_of_Limon.html

Turrialba, Cartago. (n.d.). Go Visit Costa Rica.
https://www.govisitcostarica.com/region/city.asp?cID=188

Van Velzer, R. (2023, October 23). Religion in Costa Rica. Costa Rica.
https://www.costarica.com/culture/religion-in-costa-rica

Visit Cartago: Explore Costa Rica's Beauty with LANDED Travel. (n.d.). LANDED Travel. https://landedtravel.com/destinations/cartago-turrialba/

Visiting Sarapiqui, Costa Rica: Why/When to Go & What to Do. (n.d.). Costa Rica Escapes. https://www.creescapes.com/where-to-go-in-costa-rica/heredia/sarapiqui/

Vorhees, M. (n.d.). Getting Around Costa Rica by Bus, Car, Airplane, and Boat. Lonely Planet. https://www.lonelyplanet.com/articles/how-to-get-around-costa-rica

Wangethi, I. (2023, November 12). 15 Famous People from Costa Rica Who Make Their Fellow Citizens Proud. Legit.Ng - Nigeria News. https://www.legit.ng/ask-legit/1562127-famous-people-costa-rica-fellow-citizens-proud/

Where to Stay in Costa Rica. (n.d.). Go Visit Costa Rica. https://www.govisitcostarica.com/category/hotels/accommodations.asp?rID=

Yeison. (2022, May 1). Taxis in Costa Rica: What to Know. MytanFeet. https://mytanfeet.com/about-cr/taxis-in-costa-rica-all-you-need-to-know/

Zip Line Canopy Tour from Santa Teresa. (n.d.). Monteverde Tours Costa Rica. https://monteverdetourscr.com/trip/zip-line-canopy-tour-santa-teresa-costa-rica/

Made in the USA
Monee, IL
18 December 2024